☺

The Ha-Ha Handbook

The Ha-Ha Handbook

by

Bernhard Trenkle

Zeig, Tucker & Theisen, Inc.
Phoenix, Arizona

Library of Congress Cataloging-in-Publication Data

Trenkle, Bernhard.
    [Ha-Handbuch der Psychotherapie. English]
  The ha-ha handbook / by Bernhard Trenkle.
        p. cm.
  ISBN 1-891944-47-9 (alk. paper)
    1. Psychotherapy — Humor. I. Title.

RC480.515.T7413 2001
616.89'14'0207--dc21   2001017789

Copyright © 2001 by Zeig, Tucker & Theisen, Inc.
All rights reserved. No part of this book may be reproduced by any process whatsoever without the written permission of the copyright owner.

Published by
ZEIG, TUCKER & THEISEN, INC.
3614 North 24th Street
Phoenix, AZ 85016

Manufactured in the United States of America

10 9 8 7 6 5 4 3 2 1

Contents

Preface	ix
Amnesia, Systemic Perspectives	1
The Analytical Rule	2
Anchors	3
Anthropology	5
Circular Questioning	9
Clear Boundaries Between Generations	10
Client-Centered Therapy	11
Cognitions and Self-Verbalizations	12
Common Everyday Trance	13
Conditioning	15
The Confusion Technique	16
Constructivism	19
Contact Via Nonverbal Pacing	20
Controlled Drinking	21
Counting Method	22
Deepening	23
Delegation	24
Dental Hypnosis	25
Deutero-Learning or Learning How to Learn	26
Direct Versus Indirect Communication	28
Direct Versus Indirect Hypnosis	30
Dissociation	32
Double Bind	33
Ecological Check	34
EE Studies and the Psychoeducative Approach	35
Empirical Science	36
Ethnopsychiatry and Ethnomedicine	37
Extrapunitive	38
Eye Movements: Accessing Cues	39

Focused Attention/Awareness	40
Forgetting About Amnesia	41
Future Orientation	42
Guiding Associations	44
Hallucination — Positive and Negative	45
Helper Personality	47
Homeostasis	48
Hypnosystemic Family Therapy	50
Hypnotic Speech Rhythms	52
Implications	53
Individuation — Related	54
The Inner Voice	56
Intervention	57
Intuition and Observation	59
Inward Orientation	60
The Language of the Unconscious	61
Learned Helplessness	63
Loyalty	64
Mediating	66
Meditation	67
Meeting Clients in Their Own Frames of Reference	68
Metaphoric Communication	70
Minimal Cues, and How to Read Them	72
Model Learning	74
Monoideism	75
Multiple-Level Communication	76
Multiple Partiality	77
Natural Healing Versus Modern Medicine	79
The Ordeal Technique	80
The Overlapping Technique	81
Pain Control	82
Pain Control: Dissociation and Diverting Attention	84
Part of the Whole	86
Pattern Interruption	87
Prophylaxis	88
Psychohistory	89
Psychosocial Imprinting, or Job-Related Illnesses	91
Reflexivity — Circularity — Circular Causality	93

Reframing	95
Reincarnation Therapy	98
Rigid Belief Systems and World Views	99
Role-Playing Theory of Hypnosis	100
Search Process	101
Seeding	103
Self-Hypnosis	104
Shifting of Symptoms	105
Short- Versus Long-Term Therapy	106
Side Effects	107
Stage Hypnosis	110
Strategic Therapy	111
The Structure of Magic, or "The Communication of the Masters"	113
The Structure of the Outer Interaction Becomes the Structure of the Inner Dialogue	115
Symbolism	116
Symmetric Escalation	117
Tailoring Interventions	119
Technological Advances in Medicine	120
Time	121
Triangulation	123
Turning Weaknesses Into Strengths	124
Utilization	126
Voluntary Versus Involuntary Movements	128

Preface

Primarily a joke book, *The Ha-Ha Handbook* is also a little bit more. It alludes to many of the precepts, concepts, and conceits of modern hypnosis and psychotherapy. In addition, some of the humor can be incorporated into therapy and training.

Here's how the idea came about. The Milton Erickson Gesellschaft [Institute] (MEG) is the largest society for clinical hypnosis in Germany. Named for Milton H. Erickson, pioneer in hypnotherapy and other currently used psychotherapeutic approaches, the society publishes a newsletter that goes out to about 33,000 people. In 1985, I started to include jokes in the newsletter, and soon this segment became the most popular feature of the publication, with readers eagerly anticipating a few good laughs amid some very serious material.

Once we decided to collect all of the jokes and put them in a book, we had to think about the political correctness or, more accurately, the political *in*correctness (and sometimes the downright offensiveness) of some of the jokes. Of course, many of the more tasteless jokes received the most enthusiastic feedback from our subscribers (even if the happy critics refused to sign their names to their letters). Clearly, we had a delicate matter on our hands.

In the end, we came to the conclusion that there was only one thing to do: we decided to perforate the pages of the book so that our readers could have the last word in editing its content.

I am told that in the United States, the pages crumpled up and thrown in the garbage with a gasp will be quite different from those discarded in Europe. While laughter may be a universal response, its elicitation, I realize, is various. I hope that I will not hear too many pages being torn out — I hope that you enjoy the book.

Amnesia, Systemic Perspectives

A RATHER ELDERLY MARRIED COUPLE is sitting in front of the TV set on a Monday afternoon. He is watching a rerun of a soap opera. She is trying to get him to go out and buy some ice cream. Eventually he agrees to do it. "Should I write down what I want?" she asks. He says no, but she persists: "But I want to have a banana split. Shouldn't I write it down for you?" He begins to get annoyed. "What do you take me for, an idiot?" She answers: "But I want a special kind of ice cream. I want the vanilla on the left and the chocolate on the right. There should be lots of almond chips and a few brandied cherries on top. Wouldn't it be better if I wrote it down for you?" He declines the offer repeatedly, and finally leaves. Almost an hour passes, and when he returns, carrying a grocery bag, she peers into it immediately. When she sees that the bag is full of pretzels, she becomes very upset. "I knew it," she sighs heavily, "You've forgotten the butter again."

> *For some people, forgetting certain things can have a very wholesome effect. Then again, others suffer because they are not able to forget.*

AN ANECDOTE: A ship is steering toward a small, remote island in the middle of the ocean. Standing on the island is an old man with a long white beard. The sailors call out to him. They ask whether he is a survivor of a shipwreck. The man says no, explaining that he deliberately retired to the island in order to forget. Touched by his reply, several of the crew members row over in a dinghy. They ask the old man what it is that he is trying to forget. Gazing wistfully toward the horizon, he answers: "I've forgotten."

> *Okay, forget it!*

The Analytical Rule

THE FEMALE PATIENT SAYS TO HER THERAPIST: "Kiss me, Doctor!" The therapist says: "I'm sorry, I am not allowed to do that. Actually, according to strict analytical rules, I shouldn't even be lying next to you on this couch."

Anchors

"Collapsing anchors" is a neurolinguistic programming (NLP) technique developed by John Grinder and Richard Bandler, who analyzed the communication and intervention patterns of such master therapists as Milton Erickson, Virginia Satir, and Fritz Perls. Whereas NLP seems to be somewhat marginalized in the United States, its country of origin, it is still relatively popular in Europe. In this approach, two emotional states of the client are conditioned, or anchored, to separate stimuli. Later, these two emotional states are connected with each other. For instance, a fearful frame of mind gets anchored, as well as a fearless and confident one. After collapsing the two, it should be possible for the client to access the fearless and confident state where the fearful state used to reign. The following story shows how this technique can be applied in a creative manner.

AN ATTRACTIVE WOMAN IS TRAVELING BY TRAIN. A man takes a seat in her compartment and looks at the woman, who appears to be working on some scientific papers. "Are you also going to Berlin?" he asks.
 "No, to a conference in Leipzig."
 "That's interesting. What kind of a conference is it?"
 "A conference on sexology," answers the woman.
 "That's very fascinating. What will you be doing there?"
 "I'm giving a speech on the results of my scientific research."
 "A speech on your results! And what were they actually?"
 "Well, they were very interesting," answers the researcher, "I've been researching the sexual behavior of men in different cultures."
 "How intriguing. The sexual behavior of men in different cultures. And what exactly did you find out?"
 "The main result, according to my research, was that Polish men have the longest penises and American Indians have the most staying power. But enough about me. What about you? What line of work are you in?"
 "Oh, please excuse me. How thoughtless of me. I haven't even introduced myself. My name is Kowalski, uh . . . Tecumseh Kowalski."

Another joke comes to mind.

WHILE TRAVELING OUT WEST, the talented only son of a distinquished Jewish family meets and falls in love with a beautiful young American Indian woman, and they decide to get married. His parents, especially his mother, are shocked and upset, not only because of his choice of a wife, but also because he has left law school and is moving to the reservation. His parents at first refuse to have any contact with the couple. Then, a year later, the son calls and his mother answers the phone. "Mama," the son says, "I just wanted to tell you that you are a grandmother. We have a beautiful baby boy." The mother's heart begins to melt. She completely softens when her son adds: "And we have given him a good Jewish name." "What is his name?" the mother asks excitedly. Proudly, the son replies: "Smoked Whitefish."

Anthropology

According to Milton Erickson, to become a good psychotherapist, one should study anthropology. Having an eye for different perspectives in different cultures can make one more alert to idiosyncratic views in one's own culture.

The relevance of this subject can be seen in all those jokes that rely on caricaturing the differences among nations and races.

SEVERAL ANTHROPOLOGISTS DECIDE TO CARRY OUT AN EXPERIMENT. They take three groups, each consisting of two men and a woman — a French, an English, and a Russian trio — to separate, solitary islands and leave them there. Five years later, the anthropologists return to the islands to see how things have developed. On the French island, they find all three living in a lovely house. One of the men has married the woman, the other is her lover, and life on the island has worked out fine. On the English island, they find three separate houses widely scattered. The three inhabitants have very little social contact because the anthropologists neglected to introduce them to one another at the beginning of the experiment. On the Russian island, the scientists find a blockhouse. The two men are sitting in front of it, drinking tea, and having a discussion. The scientists inquire about the woman. "Woman?" one of the men exclaims, surprised. "Our people are working in the field."

Recently, I was informed that a follow-up study to this field experiment had been conducted. This time, the experiment also included Italian, German, Greek, and Irish trios. On the Italian island, the scientists discovered only one person, one of the men. He had shot his two companions in a jealous rage. On the Greek island, the two men had formed an intimate relationship and the woman dropped in every now and then to share recipes and gossip. The Irish had divided the island into a northern and a southern section and had built a distillery. The word "sex" had disappeared completely as everything evaporated into a light fog after the first few quarts of liquor. One thing was clear, however: the English on the neighboring island wouldn't be supplied with whiskey. On the island where the Germans lived, everything worked according to schedule: the men had created a detailed daily agenda regulating every activity — including who had a right to the woman, and when.

WHAT IS THE DIFFERENCE BETWEEN A FRENCH, AN ENGLISH, AND A GERMAN PENSIONER? The English pensioner visits the racetrack in the mornings and his pub at midday. The French pensioner seeks out his bistro in the mornings and his girlfriend at midday. The German pensioner takes his heart medication in the mornings and goes to work at midday.

I heard the following joke for the first time toward the end of 1992, when the economic situation in Germany was starting to change for the worse. People were becoming aware of the problems arising from financing a united Germany. Many employers were transferring their businesses to Hungary or Czechoslovakia where wages were lower. This joke mirrors not only some national peculiarities and prejudices, but also aspects of European economic realities at the time.

SAINT PETER'S DOOR TO HEAVEN BREAKS, so he makes a public announcement to ask who will repair Heaven's door and offer a discount for the work without skimping on its quality? Three firms bid for the job, one from Germany, one from Poland, and one from Italy. The German estimate is 30,000; the Polish company comes in at 5,000; and the Italians bid 25,000. As the differences among the three estimates are too great to simply choose the cheapest one, Saint Peter decides that the three entrepreneurs should explain their estimates in detail.

First, he summons the German: "Look, I've received three different offers. Yours is by far the most expensive. Why?" The German answers: "That's German quality you are paying for. Such precision has its price. On top of that, we have high labor costs, and we pay higher church taxes than our competitors do. I would only use the very best materials for Heaven's door and high-quality wood is expensive. In addition, transport to Heaven is no trivial matter. So one can say it's 10,000 for the material, 10,000 for the transport, and 10,000 for the labor."

This sounds plausible to Saint Peter, and he asks the Polish master craftsman to appear before him: "Listen, I've received different offers. Yours is by far the cheapest. But I find myself hesitating a bit." The Pole answers: "As far as the quality is concerned, you needn't worry. We have very large forests where I can get good quality wood — it's not really stolen — but I get it very inexpensively. Moreover, my brother-in-law will drive it to Heaven secretly in a company truck on the weekend. The rest we will manage for 5,000."

Finally, Saint Peter calls the Italian: "Listen, I've received three different offers. Yours isn't the most expensive, but I've also received a significantly better offer. How do you calculate your estimate?" The Italian leans toward Saint Peter and whispers: "10,000 for you, 10,000 for me, and I have a Polish man who will do the job for 5,000."

IN COMMENTING ON THE BILL CLINTON/MONICA LEWINSKY EPISODE, the German politician Karsten Voigt made the following statement. "In France, it's one's duty as a politician to have an affair; in America, a politician is not allowed to have an affair; and in Germany, thank Heavens, it's still voluntary."

> *The joke about Saint Peter and Heaven's door reminds me of a joke that a Polish friend, Peter, told me.*
>
> *We were on a tour following a week of seminars in the Polish monastery of Wigry. I'd placed my old Opel Kadett, already showing close to 150,000 miles on the odometer, at everyone's disposal. Peter returned from a shopping expedition and I noticed at once that my car's gas tank cap was missing. Peter was both dismayed and embarrassed. We tucked an old rag into the opening as a makeshift plug and Peter drove off to look for the cap or a replacement. He returned with a loosely fitting cap from a Ford and then told me the following joke.*

EVERY NEWCOMER TO HEAVEN has to pass an entrance examination given by Saint Peter. The first to arrive at Heaven's door is a Frenchman. Saint Peter hands him two large, perfectly shaped stainless steel globes. The Frenchman builds a mobile, with the globes incorporated in a weightless way. Saint Peter comments: "Ah, that's French elegance. You are allowed to enter." Next to show up is a German. He also is handed the two steel balls. He puts one on the table and sets the other on top of it. The second globe stays in place on the first one. Saint Peter is astonished and says: "That's German precision. You may enter Heaven." Next to arrive is a Pole. Saint Peter also gives him the two steel balls. The Pole breaks one of the globes and loses the other.

> *My old car's odometer now registers 180,000 miles — and putting the new cap on the tank whenever I fill it still makes me smile, three years later.*

SPEAKING OF TRANSPORTATION: Two Israelis board a train and find that the only available seats are in a compartment occupied by two Arabs. The atmosphere at first is very tense, but after a while the four start conversing, with the high price of the train fare a welcome neutral topic. The two Israelis mention that to beat the system, they always purchase only one ticket between the two of them. The Arabs doubt that this ruse can be successful given the vigilance of the train conductors. The Israelis shrug and tell them to wait and see what happens. A short time later, a call from the other end of the car can be heard: "Tickets please!" The two Israelis get up and disappear into the toilet. After a while, the conductor checks the Arabs' tickets and then moves on to the toilet, which is locked. "Your ticket please!" The two Israelis slide their one ticket under the door, and the conductor punches it and proceeds to the next compartment. A week later, the four happen to meet again on the platform and find a compartment together. The Arabs thank the Israelis for the tip about the train tickets and tell them that this time they also have purchased only one ticket for both of them. All listen intently so that they can hear the conductor approach. Eventually, the call can be heard: "Tickets please." The two Arabs rush to the toilet and disappear into the stall. A moment passes. There is a knock on the door of the toilet. "Tickets please!" says one of the Israelis.

Circular Questioning

This systemic family therapy technique was developed in the 1970s. It involves complex questions posed to a family, such as: "Let's suppose Grandma is there: What would Grandma say Mom feels like when the daughter starts eating again and the father starts concentrating on his job once again?"

THE SITUATION RESPONSIBLE FOR THE DEVELOPMENT of this multilayered mixture of giving and getting information is less well known. Mara Selvini was returning to Milan from a psychoanalytic conference in Zurich. At first, she was the only passenger in her compartment. Then she was joined by a young Sicilian man and, somewhat later, by a woman accompanied by her beautiful 18-year-old daughter. Finally, a businessman from northern Italy arrived, and glancing disdainfully at his fellow countryman, took a seat in the compartment, which had become quite crowded. After a while, the train entered a tunnel, and in the dark compartment, the sound of someone kissing could be heard, followed by the sound of a slap. When the train emerged from the tunnel, a red blotch such as would be caused by a slap was clearly visible on the northern Italian's cheek. An icy silence prevailed. The daughter left the compartment and Mara Selvini followed her to find out what had actually happened. The daughter said that she wasn't sure, but suspects that the man had tried to kiss her, but had kissed her mother by mistake, and she had slapped him. Then when the mother left the compartment, Mara asked her for her version of the incident, and she said: "He must have tried to kiss my daughter and she slapped him. I didn't believe she was capable of it." As Mara started back to her seat, rather perplexed, she passed the businessman on his way to the lavatory to cool his stinging cheek. "I know it's none of my business," she said, "but what really happened?" "That impertinent young Sicilian must have tried to kiss the daughter, and she, thinking it was me, gave me a slap." When Mara entered the compartment, she found the Sicilian there alone, and she looked at him with a questioning expression. He winked at her and said, with a broad smile: "When they're all back and we pass through another tunnel, I'll click my tongue again and that arrogant snob will get another slap on the cheek."

It was during this journey that Mara started wondering whether her single questioning technique might be too elaborate and inefficient — and this marked the beginning of systemic family therapy and circular questioning.

Clear Boundaries Between Generations

The structural family therapy approach (Minuchin), as well as the strategic approach (Haley), emphasizes the need for clear hierarchies for the functioning of families. In other words, it must be clear who the parents are and who the children are.

The following anecdote from Isaac Asimov shows this mechanism and possible therapeutic interventions in a simple and yet expressive way.

After lengthy negotiations, union representatives and the owner of a firm reached an agreement on a pension plan for the employees, but only on condition that all personnel, without exception, agree and sign the contract within one month. All of the staff members signed the contract, except for Paul, who was in charge of the stockroom. He complained that the whole thing was too complicated for him, he didn't understand the meaning of it all and couldn't see the advantages, and anyway he didn't like signing things that he didn't understand. His colleagues, his superiors, the union representatives, all tried to get him to sign, but to no avail. The deadline for accepting the agreement was approaching, and the contract that had been so laboriously hammered out was in danger. Finally, the president of the firm summoned Paul to his office. A pen and the contract were lying on the desk. The executive began: "I know and appreciate your work for our company over the years. And with regard to what I am about to tell you, I can assure you that I have the support of your colleagues and your union. Now, as you know, we are in my office on the sixth floor. If you have not signed this contract by the time I have counted to 10, I am going to throw you out of this window, and the countdown starts now: one, two, three ..." Paul grabbed the pen and calmly signed, with no evidence of being perturbed. The president carefully folded the signed document and asked: "My good man, with all due respect, why didn't you sign this contract earlier?" Paul's answer: "You were the first one to explain it to me clearly."

Client-Centered Therapy

In the psychotherapeutic method introduced by Carl Rogers, much importance is placed on empathic communication, whereby the therapist mirrors the client's feelings.

The following story shows the extent of intensive empathy possible when the principle of mirroring what the client says is consistently maintained.

Client: "I just feel profoundly sad."
Therapist: "You just feel profoundly sad."
Client: "All of life is so meaningless and everything is like a black hole."
Therapist: "Life is so meaningless and everything seems black."
Client: "It is like a maelstrom. All I can really still do is kill myself."
Therapist: "It is like a maelstrom. Actually all you can still do is kill yourself."
Client gets up without a word, slowly walks to the window, opens it, and jumps.
Therapist: "Splat."

The following example also shows the intense contact that can result when two people reciprocally adjust to each other's mentality.

TWO FRIENDS MEET BY CHANCE in the street after not having seen each other for some time. They exchange news about the happenings in their lives since their last encounter a few years earlier and the following dialogue ensues.
Friend 1: "Yes, I got married ten months ago, but then my wife died four weeks ago."
Friend 2: "How tragic! What did she have?"
Friend 1: "A small shop and a few thousand dollars in the bank.
Friend 2: "No, that's not what I meant. What was wrong with her?"
Friend 1: "Oh, right. Well she had neither a building site nor the money to expand her business."
Friend 2: "No, I don't mean that either. What did she die of?"
Friend 1: "Oh I see. Well she went into the cellar to fetch a few potatoes for dinner, fell, and broke her neck."
Friend 2: "Good Heavens! What did you do?"
Friend 1: "I made spaghetti instead."

Cognitions and Self-Verbalizations

Cognitive therapists and hypnotherapists observe inner dialogues and include what the clients say to themselves (e.g., "I'll never be able to do that") in the therapeutic process.

Members of other professions are also increasingly learning strategies that were developed by the psychotherapeutic profession.

This judge seems to have had interdisciplinary training. He is trying to reach a better understanding of the events leading up to a bank robbery by including a witness's cognitive impressions.

THE JUDGE ASKS THE WITNESS: "So what you're saying is that you saw how the defendant stormed into the bank pointing a gun?" The witness answers in the affirmative. The judge continues: "Where were you standing at the time?" The witness says that he was standing on the opposite sidewalk, about 30 feet away from the entrance to the bank. The judge goes on: "And the idea of calling the police didn't occur to you? Just what exactly were you thinking of?" The witness: "Well I can't remember exactly, but I think it was something like uh oh, uh oh, uh oh . . . !"

Common Everyday Trance

Common everyday trance is a concept of Ericksonian hypnotherapy, which maintains that spontaneous trance states take place throughout the day. The experienced hypnotherapist can identify these states whenever a client lapses into them during a therapy session and can then work with them in a therapeutic manner.

The following story proves that Richard von Weizsäcker, president of Germany from 1984 to 1994, also knew about spontaneous trances.

SOME YEARS AGO, the Pope visited Germany and gave a dinner party to which dignitaries of the church and state were invited. Cardinal Höffner, the most eminent representative of the German church, sat on the Pope's right. Richard von Weizsäcker sat on his left, and next to him sat Helmut Kohl, the German chancellor. A beautiful set of antique silverware from the Vatican Museum adorned the table. While the Pope, deeply absorbed in a common everyday trance, was in the middle of a conversation with Cardinal Höffner concerning the appointment of a candidate for the bishop's chair, Kohl and von Weizsäcker whispered admiringly about the lovely dessert spoons. It would be too much to hope, they agreed, that they might be given a spoon as a souvenir, as not even the Pope was entitled to relinquish them. Noticing that the Pope was still in deep conversation with Höffner, during a moment in which the Pope seemed to be fully absorbed in his thoughts, von Weizsäcker reached over and took one of the spoons. Without haste, he put it in his left trouser pocket and winked impishly at Kohl, but Kohl failed to see the humor. After all, von Weizsäcker was in possession of one of the treasured spoons and he himself was not. Kohl had noticed how von Weizsäcker had managed to obtain the desired object by taking advantage of a moment when the Pope had gone into a short trance. Kohl watched the Pope, and soon the Pope seemed again to be completely absent for a minute. Quickly, Kohl reached across von Weizsäcker, but in doing so knocked against von Weizsäcker's glass, producing a clear, resounding ring that attracted everyone's attention. Whether he wanted to or not, he had to make a speech. A short while later, another opportunity arose. Once again, Kohl quickly reached across von Weizsäcker and once again bumped against the latter's glass and was forced to make another speech. Kohl didn't want to risk this maneuver a third time. He pondered his problem. Finally, he turned to the Pope and steered the conversation toward hobbies. He knew that the Pope and von Weizsäcker were both sports fans, so they talked about sports for a while. Just as Kohl thought he would, the Pope, in turn, asked Kohl: "Do you also go in for sports, Chancellor Kohl, or do you have other hobbies?"

"Oh yes," answered Kohl. "I used to play football when I was young, but my real hobby was magic."

"Really?" said the Pope, amazed. "Can you still perform magic tricks?"

"Not many," Kohl replied. With the Pope, as well as Höffner, von Weizsäcker, and the others, encouraging him to perform one of the tricks from his repertoire, he consented, but on one condition, that he would perform only one trick. He began: "Now I will take, for example, this wonderful little spoon lying before the Holy Father. As everyone can see, I am placing it in the inside pocket of my jacket. And from where do I remove the spoon? Why, right here, from the president's trouser pocket . . ."

Children love this joke.

Conditioning

Conditioning, a term often used in classical behavior therapy, implies the development of conditions through learning processes, intended or not (e.g., new stimulus-reaction combinations or reaction-anticipation combinations), that formerly (i.e., as reflexes) had not existed. The methods used for their verification — experiments on animals and studies conducted in laboratories — led not only to a discussion concerning the validity of the outcome when applied to human beings in everyday life, but also to several jokes. The "Harvard Law of General Behavior" was published in the 1960s: "Under highly controlled conditions, laboratory animals do just what they want to do." The emancipation of laboratory animals is reflected in the conversation taking place between two rats in Skinner's laboratory:

"THESE LEARNING PRINCIPLES ARE FANTASTIC. Everytime I press a lever, the guy in the white coat has to feed me."

The ethical and specific human problems that arise when applying modes of animal reactions to more highly developed species are made obvious — even if on a different level — by the following story.

AN AMERICAN BIG-GAME HUNTER was following Ernest Hemingway's footsteps deep in the heart of Africa. A lioness, backed into a corner by this hunter, didn't know what else to do other than bite off the most precious symbol of his manhood. Luckily, a member of the safari was a surgeon. In order to save as much as possible, he patched up the wound with the trunk of a newly killed elephant. Against all odds, the operation was successful. A few years later, the surgeon happened to meet the former patient and asked him how he was doing. "Oh," he answered, "I'm fine, no complications whatsoever. I only have to keep away from those little bowls of peanuts at parties." (Note: Karl Ludwig Holtz, professor of pedagogic and child psychology in Heidelberg, contributed this joke.)

HERE IS ANOTHER JOKE ABOUT CONDITIONING: "I wanted to train my dog to bark whenever he is hungry. I repeated the exercise more than 200 times. The result is that he does not eat as long I am not barking."

The Confusion Technique

Erickson saw the confusion technique as one of his most important contributions to the field of hypnosis. (Note: For an excellent article about the confusion technique, see: Rossi, E. [1980]. The Collected Papers of Milton Erickson. New York: Irvington. Also, Stephen Gilligan writes about the approach in Therapeutic Trances.) By applying this method, the conscious mode of thought is overloaded or overcharged with an abundance of illogical and contradictory messages, which is why it is also sometimes called the "overload technique." The trance and search processes are thereby set in motion. Once Erickson rounded a corner and bumped into a man. Before the man could say anything, Erickson looked at his watch and said: "It's exactly 10 to 2."

In fact, the time was 4 o'clock. Erickson continued on his way for a while. When he looked back, he saw the man still glued to the same spot, motionless.

Anyway, someone once said: "Before every enlightenment, there is some confusion." (Note: Jay Haley gave a lecture on the parallels between Zen and strategic therapy at the 1990 Evolution of Psychotherapy Conference. See Haley, J. [1993]. Jay Haley on Milton Erickson. New York: Brunner/Mazel.)

A classic example of the application of the confusion technique comes from Germany's Black Forest.

A MAN IN A RESTAURANT orders a piece of Black Forest cake. When it arrives, he beckons to the waitress and tells her that it isn't fresh. She apologizes and brings him a slice of cheesecake instead. The man eats his cheesecake, gets up, and leaves. The waitress runs after him and calls out: "You didn't pay for your cheesecake." The man answers: "Why should I? I gave back the Black Forest cake in exchange." The waitress says: "Yes, but you didn't pay for that either." The man: "Why should I? I didn't eat it."

The story goes that when the man turned around to look back, the waitress was standing motionless, rooted to the spot.

THEN THERE'S THE ABSTRACT PAINTER who is explaining one of his works of art he calls: "Cows in a Meadow." "But I don't see any grass," one viewer remarks. The artist answers:

"The cows have already eaten it." The viewer: "I don't see any cows either." The artist: "Perhaps you could explain to me what cows would be doing in a meadow where the grass has already been eaten."

This is a simple triggering of search processes and making use of mild confusion. Another artist was comissioned to paint a "really" surrealistic picture — a difficult task, thought the artist. When the painting was unveiled, the client was visibly disappointed and confused. The picture showed in great detail a path that led into a forest. It was painted with such precision that it was possible to make out every blade of grass. It looked like a photograph. "That's not a surrealistic picture," the client complained. "So, is that what you think?" was the artist's rejoinder, whereupon he stepped onto the path leading to the forest, becoming smaller and smaller until, finally, he disappeared into the forest itself.

IMAGINE THAT PORSCHE DRIVER'S FEELINGS as he stops at a red traffic light early one morning. A jogger stops next to him, a challenging look in his eyes. The driver of the Porsche occasionally revs up the engine, the jogger provokingly runs on the spot. The traffic light turns yellow, then green. Both speed on their way. The jogger disappears into the horizon, clearly in the lead, when suddenly a mushroom cloud appears in the middle of the street. The driver barely manages to come to a stop at the edge of a smoking crater. In the middle of the crater sits the somewhat dazed jogger. The driver asks: "Are you hurt?" The jogger answers: "You're a fine one to ask. Have you ever had a running shoe burst doing 160 mph?"

But "really hypnotized surrealistically?" Two cows are sitting in a cellar, chopping wood. "Tomorrow is Whitsunday" says one. The other answers: "I know, but I'm not going. I'm just visiting."
And now a little something on the practical employment of the confusion technique in everyday life:

A MAN ON HIS WAY SOMEWHERE sees an attractive woman and says: "Excuse me, but didn't we meet last year in New York?" She answers: "I'm sorry, I've never been to New York." The man: "I've never been to New York either, so it must have been an entirely different pair."

HOW TO REACT TO CONFUSION PROPERLY was demonstrated by Saint Peter a few years ago while playing golf with God. God spoiled his tee-off, and the ball rolled in the direction of the sandtrap when along came a mouse and snatched the ball. A cat appeared and grabbed the mouse. An eagle dropped out of the sky, picked up the cat, and swooped skyward. A flash of lightning struck the eagle holding the cat, which was clutching the mouse with the golf ball, and the golf ball dropped right into the hole. Saint Peter turned to God and said: "What's it to be? Are we playing golf or just fooling around?"

Constructivism

This philosophy implies that there is no such thing as reality per se, only views of "reality."

A NEUROLOGIST, AN ORTHOPEDIST, AND A PSYCHIATRIST are taking a stroll. On the other side of the street, they see a man walking with a very peculiar gait. The neurologist says: "That's clearly a case of cerebral palsy. Just look at the typical scissor-like movement!"

The orthopedist interjects: "That is a completely false diagnosis. That man is suffering from the Marie Strumpfel syndrome."

The psychiatrist disagrees with both diagnoses: "That's typical of physicians. Whenever you see a bodily defect, you assume the cause must be organic in origin. No, his problem is hysteric in nature."

The three can't seem to agree, and finally decide to bet a large sum of money. They approach — although a bit apprehensively — the man with the funny gait, who has stopped and is gazing about searchingly. When asked, the man doesn't seem to have a problem with the question: "Nice of you to approach me. I'm a doctor myself and I can give you the correct diagnosis. All I can say is this, if I don't find a toilet soon . . ."

(Note: This joke is from Harold Mosak's Haha and Aha: The Use of Humor in Psychotherapy. *Muncie, IN: Accelerated Development, one of the best books about the use of humor in psychotherapy. It contains an excellent collection of jokes related to psychotherapy and its practitioners.)*

Contact Via Nonverbal Pacing

Pacing comes from to pace and means "to keep abreast of someone, to fall into step with someone." The term was introduced by J. Grinder and R. Bandler. The pacing strategy they recommended included, among other things, adopting the same body posture as the client or breathing in the same rhythm. This procedure results in better contact with the client. However, it was not known until recently how this strategy actually works, and that it is also employed in Paradise.

JESUS IS MAKING HIS ROUNDS IN PARADISE. Everyone is having a really good time. Only one person, an elderly man, is sitting hunched over in a corner, looking depressed. At first, Jesus wants to talk to him but then thinks better of it, saying to himself that perhaps that's the way the man enjoys Paradise. But when Jesus sees the old man still sitting there a week later, he sits down next to him and starts breathing in the same rhythm. Eventually, he starts talking to the man: "You are in Paradise. You can eat and drink, play musical instruments, amuse yourself, do whatever your heart desires . . ." The old man sighs and says: "You know, I was a carpenter on earth, and it is my heart's desire to meet my son again in Heaven."

Tears spring to Jesus' eyes. He embraces the old man, sobbing: "Papa!"

The old man's eyes also fill with tears: "Pinocchio!"

Controlled Drinking

One of the controversial themes in addiction therapy is whether alcoholics are capable of controlling their drinking. The following story illustrates the concept.

THREE FRIENDS MAKE THE ROUNDS FROM ONE BAR TO ANOTHER, drinking heavily. Finally, they settle down in one and continue their spree with fervor. Eventually, one of them topples off his stool as if in slow motion and comes to rest on the floor. One of the two still sitting on their stools says to the other: "You have to say one thing for him. He really knows when to stop."

The following story is also appropriate here.

A MAN ENTERS A NEIGHBORHOOD RESTAURANT and orders three beers. The waitress asks whether more guests are expected. The man says no and explains that one of the beers is for his brother in France and one is for his brother in the United States.

Later, he visits the restaurant again and orders another three beers, and this routine continues for a couple of weeks. One day, he comes into the restaurant and orders only two beers. The room suddenly becomes quiet and the concerned waitress softly inquires: "Has anything happened to one of your brothers?" The man explains: "No, but I've stopped drinking." (Note: Andreas, my 12-year-old [at the time] son, told me this joke, and insisted that I had to cite him.)

To what extent alcohol was involved in the loss of control outlined in the following accident report is not clear. "... then I took the corner at high speed, shot across the lane, crashed into a garden fence, and turned over three times. Finally, I lost control of my car."

Counting Method

Some hypnotherapists use a counting method to deepen the trance state: "And I will count to 20, and with each number, you will sink deeper and deeper into trance . . ." Some people use this counting method for self-hypnosis inductions, as the following story shows.

Two colleagues attending a conference on hypnosis are sitting at the hotel bar at 11 p.m. Much to the other's astonishment, one of them drinks several cups of coffee, causing his companion to ask: "Can you still fall asleep after all that coffee?" The coffee drinker answers: "No problem, I've got my own method. I use a mixture consisting of a strict ritual combined with a counting technique, and I religiously follow the same procedure no matter where I am. First, I undress, then I always play the same piece of music, then I go into the bathroom to brush my teeth, and then I look out of the window for exactly two minutes. I turn off the music, put out the light, go to bed, and count to two, and then I fall asleep."
"You only count to two? After all that coffee? Does it always work?"
"Well, okay," his colleague admits, "sometimes I count to half past three."

Deepening

The experienced hypnotherapist knows several different ways to increase or deepen the trance state. Some directly suggest a deepening of the trance: "You are going deeper and deeper into trance. You are sinking deeper, ever deeper." Other therapists prefer to use images, such as walking down steps into a pool of warm water. Still others use stories and metaphors to indirectly suggest a deepening of the trance. The following story interspersed with suggestions should be utilized only by very experienced hypnotherapists as a technique to deepen the trance state.

HEAD FORESTER FOX IS SITTING WITH SOME PROFESSIONAL COLLEAGUES. The jargon is becoming more esoteric as the evening wears on and eventually Fox decides to relate an experience: "My most intensive hunting experience was in the fall of 1983. I was following the track of a 12-point stag. The hunt had been going on for an entire day. I'd lost track of time [time distortion]. Night fell abruptly and soon it was quite dark. I couldn't find my way and got caught in a swamp. I can tell you, I was slowly sinking deeper and deeper. I was stuck in the bog right up to my hips and yet I was still sinking deeper and deeper. I began to cry for help, but who could hear me out there? So I sank ever deeper and deeper."

"And," his colleagues ask him, spellbound: "Who found you and saved you?"

The forester: "Nobody. I drank."

Delegation

The concept of delegation was introduced into family therapy by Helm Stierlin. A delegate is someone sent out by a family to fulfill a task, tethered by the long leash of loyalty (e.g., to become a famous scientist or to become a feminist in order to take vengeance for the exploitation of one's mother). (Note: Helm Stierlin, the dean and pioneer of German family therapy, lived in the United States for 17 years and worked at various prestigious places, including the National Institute of Mental Health. In his book about Adolf Hitler, you can find what is perhaps the best description of the delegation concept. His mother lived in the little village of Eppelheim, near Heidelberg. It is just a nice conceit that Stierlin developed this idea while traveling to visit his mother.)

What is not commonly known, though, is that an American family by the name of Brown was mostly responsible for the concept. In Heidelberg, the Browns, who were tourists, took a tram going in the direction of Eppelheim. Stierlin, who had just arrived from the United States on home leave, got on the same tram to visit his mother. The following short dialogue took place among an elderly Bavarian woman, the Brown family, and Helm Stierlin.

THE WOMAN SAID TO MRS. BROWN, in her Bavarian dialect: "You really have two sweet sons. How old are they?"

Mrs. Brown: "Sorry, but I don't understand you."

Stierlin, intervening: "This lady admires your boys. She is asking their ages."

Mrs. Brown: "Oh, how nice. You can tell her that the lawyer is three and the doctor is four and a half."

The Bavarian woman was waiting for an answer, but Stierlin seemed completely absorbed. He philosophized about his medical studies, almost forgot to get off the tram in front of his mother's house, and developed his concept of delegation shortly afterward.

Dental Hypnosis

This is a special application of hypnosis that 80% of the dentists in Sweden utilize. In the United States, it is employed by only a few, very brave dental practitioners. (Note: I myself have had three wisdom teeth extracted in 20 minutes with hypnotic anesthesia only. This took place in the morning. In the afternoon, I was seeing clients again. There was neither swelling nor pain.)
The event that discredited dental hypnosis, however, is not well known.

A HYPNOSIS ASSISTANT HYPNOTIZED A PATIENT who was sitting in the dental chair, waiting to undergo a painful procedure. As soon as the woman had reached a satisfactory trance state, the dentist, who had been attending to another patient in the meantime, was so informed. The assistant continued: "... and while you hear the doctor entering the room, you can sink deeper and deeper into trance with every step he takes, and your left hand can rise ever higher." The assistant concentrated on the arm levitation and finally suggested that the patient's mouth relax and her jaws open. The doctor began to bend over the patient. Suddenly, the hypnosis assistant noticed that the doctor had gone into a state of cataleptic rigidity. She had seldom seen such a sudden change from one state of consciousness to another. Then she saw that the patient had a tight grip on the doctor's most treasured parts, and she heard her say, very softly: "Doctor, you and I aren't going to hurt each other now, are we?" And since then, this lack of trust in hypnosis, in view of the fact that a certain degree of hypnotic trance had been apparent in the patient, has penetrated the deepest layers of the dental community.

Deutero-Learning or Learning How to Learn

It is possible to learn and to learn how to learn. Simply learning is first-order learning and learning how to learn is second-order learning. Gregory Bateson called second-order learning deutero-learning. Idries Shah, author and Sufi, has written an excellent book entitled Learning How to Learn.
The following story addresses this concept.

A MAN GOES TO SEE A RABBI, and asks: "Rabbi, what is meant by an alternative?"

The rabbi hesitates and carefully studies the face of the questioner.

He begins to answer: "An alternative? That is not an easy question. It's best to give you an example. Just imagine you have a hen. You can slaughter this hen and you can have soup or fried chicken. Of course, you can also wait and you will have an egg."

"Aha!" the man says and his face registers a look of enlightenment. "That is an alternative."

"But wait," the rabbi says, "the story isn't over. Just imagine you have decided to wait for an egg. So you will have a hen and an egg. Chickens are animals you can eat after they die and before they are born. Of course, you can eat the egg. But you can also wait until a baby chick is born. Then you will have two chickens."

Again the look of enlightenment: "Aha! That is an altern...."

The rabbi interrupts him: "Just a moment. That is not the end of the story. Just imagine that you always opt for breeding. Just imagine. After a while, you will have eight chickens, then 20 chickens, and eventually perhaps more than 100 chickens. With so many chickens, you can start a chicken farm. With a chicken farm, other possibilities open up. You can start the business close to your home. You are always there, you always have fresh eggs, and you are in control of the whole thing. Of course, you may find the smell unpleasant. So, instead, you can start your chicken farm in a river valley, where the chickens will always have fresh water and green grass. But, of course, you are not there. Perhaps one morning you arrive and find that, during the night, a fox has been there and all the chickens are dead."

"Aha! That is an ...." the man tries to say.

"Just a moment. Why so impatient? The story has not ended yet. Just imagine you have decided to establish the business in the river valley. Just imagine this. Conditions are ideal, the business is growing and growing. You have 200 chickens, 500 chickens, and in the end, more than 1,000 chickens. You have built a thriving business and you are very proud of it. But then it starts to rain. And it rains and rains and rains. Endless rain. The river gets higher and higher and floods the farm, and all the chickens die."

The rabbi stops talking and sits there silently.

The man waits, but seems confused: "But what is the alternative?"

The rabbi smiles: "Ducks, my friend. Ducks!

Direct Versus Indirect Communication

One of the topics of current interest in the field is whether direct or indirect suggestions have a better therapeutic effect. The existential meaning that any knowledge on this subject could have becomes apparent in the following situation concerning an application for a job.

THE PROFESSOR OF MEDICINE AT THE UNIVERSITY has lost his ears. Nobody knows exactly how he lost them. Everyone just tactfully ignores the issue, and yet it's quite obvious that the professor's ears are missing.

One day, the professor interviews applicants for a job as an assistant in the clinic. The first one enters the room and the professor asks: "And? What do you observe?"

The young man thinks to himself: "If I tell him to his face that he hasn't any ears, I'll probably have lost the job already."

So he starts by mentioning the nice desk, the recent books lying there, the Picasso on the wall, and so on.

Eventually, the professor interrupts him: "My good man, and you want to become a doctor! You have absolutely no power of observation! Even a child can see that I don't have any ears. Imagine what would happen if you were to examine a patient in this clinic and fail to notice something so obvious. No, I can't have such a doctor on my team." The young doctor leaves the room but is fair and informs the two remaining applicants waiting outside how the conversation went. "The professor hasn't any ears and if you don't see that, you won't stand a chance of getting the job."

The second candidate enters the room and is asked the same question: "Well? What do you observe?"

The young woman answers: "You haven't any ears."

The professor explodes: "My goodness, how can you think of being a doctor? You have absolutely no feeling for the situation, absolutely no delicacy. You can't be so indiscreet. Imagine that you make a diagnosis and then inform the patient in this tactless manner. No, I can't do with such a doctor on my team."

The second candidate tells the third one in passing how it went. The third candidate enters the room and is asked the same question: "What do you observe?" The third young doctor answers: "You're wearing contact lenses." The professor: "Unbelievable, what powers of observation, and what a fast response! I have never seen a doctor whose response was so swift and so confident. How did you notice it so quickly?" The third candidate answers: "To be honest, I didn't see it. I deduced it. After all, glasses would slip."

The following episode also shows the strength and possibilities that can be inherent in indirect suggestions.

A DOCTOR IS STUDYING A PATIENT'S X-RAYS in the patient's presence. At the same time, he is talking to his wife on the phone: "Darling, I just found out that an apartment will be vacant very soon."

(Note: The German Milton Erickson Society of Clinical Hypnosis has started training for medical doctors, as well as for nurses, in how to avoid such implicit negative suggestions and to learn benevolent communication patterns that are supportive of the treatment and comfort of the patient.)

Direct Versus Indirect Hypnosis

The difference between direct and indirect Ericksonian hypnosis is about as great as that between man and woman. Frank Farrelly, the father of provocative therapy, once said that men and women speak different languages. The difficulties of comprehension are the same as if the man were speaking in Chinese and the woman in Swahili.

While working in Heidelberg at the university clinic a few years ago, I was one of two men among more than two dozen women. To maintain a certain basic orientation, I tried to learn "Swahili" as quickly as possible.

I never got further than a bit of initial knowledge though. Thus, I could never understand why some women never laughed at certain jokes, or sometimes even became indignant (although I tried to translate the jokes into Swahili as well as I could). I felt more regret upon hearing reports that the women told even better jokes once the men had left the room. I must have started speaking Swahili without much of an accent after a while for the following story to be related to me while I was the only man in a small gathering of women.

A speech therapist said to me: "You work with hypnosis, don't you? Should I tell you a hypnosis joke?" At the time, I was still of the opinion that she should. [Last warning: when relating this joke, men and women should be split up into two separate groups, as, according to my devoted studies of many years, jokes in this class can only be appreciated if men and women are among themselves.]

A MAN IS WALKING THROUGH A PARK and sees an attractive woman sitting on a bench. He slowly approaches the bench and gazes deep into the woman's eyes, moves his hands in a certain manner, and starts talking slowly and rhythmically: "And you will accompany me, and you don't know it!" [I do regret it, but the hand movements are nonverbal hypnosis techniques for advanced scholars and not for everybody — otherwise every student or teacher would go into the park and abuse these techniques, which are reserved for doctors and psychologists schooled in hypnosis.] Anyway, the woman gets up and accompanies the man. When they arrive at his house, he gazes deep into her eyes once again and says: "And you will accompany me, and you don't know it." Once inside his apartment, the man follows up his suggestions with: "And you will undress and you don't know it." The woman follows his instructions, and eventually he says: "And you will sleep with me and you won't know it." After they sleep together, the young man suddenly says: "You were in trance, weren't you? Or not? That can't be? You wanted to sleep with me, didn't you?" The young woman gazes deep into his eyes, makes the same typical movements of her hand [that we are, alas, still not allowed to describe] and says in a slow, rhythmic way: "And you are now infected with gonorrhea and you don't know it."

> *I was so shocked at this direct sledgehammer method that I turned to the speech therapist and said: "Well yes, that is the old, traditional form of hypnosis — direct suggestions, authoritarian style, and so on. I'll tell you what modern Ericksonian hypnosis is about: you work with indirect approaches, with implications, with pictures; one stimulates the imagination and respects, activates, and utilizes the other's needs. It goes something like this:*

A MAN IS SITTING IN A BAR ONE EVENING and watches a rather unattractive man come through the door and gaze around the room. His eyes light on a pretty young woman. He approaches her, and after a moment, the woman gets up, hastily pays her tab, and follows him outside. The next evening, the same thing happens again: the young man gives the barroom a cursory glance, makes his choice, approaches a woman, and leaves the bar with her a short time later. The observer becomes more curious with each passing evening. Finally, one evening he waits at the entrance, and when the stranger appears, he approaches him and says: "I've been watching you for a few days now. You enter, look around, go to a woman, and say or do something and the woman just follows you. Why?"

The man answers: "Oh, that's easy: I smooth out my eyebrows with my tongue and ask her: 'Shall we go?' "

> *(Note: As an afterthought, I would like to say that I look back with satisfaction on that moment in New York when, after some reflection, I decided to invest in a collection of the complete Playboy party jokes for 1952–1968. Who knows whether I'd have been able to portray indirect methods in such a vivid, sensitive manner otherwise.)*

Dissociation

When part of an experience has been separated from the whole, we speak of dissociation. In a trance, for instance, parts of the body can be experienced as being dissociated or a part of experiencing of feelings can be perceived as being split off. The following story shows how training can enhance this ability to dissociate until it becomes fully developed.

Two former hypnotherapists, both with long histories of experience with hetero- and autohypnosis, dropped out a few years ago and are traveling around the country as hoboes. Suddenly, they spot a human leg, which must have been ripped off, lying at the side of the road. "Nice, nice," says one cooly. The two ramble on. A short distance further, they notice the other leg. A little further still, they happen on a hand, and then an arm. The two continue to wander along at a leisurely pace. Finally, at the side of the road, they spy a head, lying face downward. The one in front turns the head face up and exclaims: "Jeez, it's Charlie! Let's hope nothing has happened to him!"

(Note: An alternative punch line might be: "Charlie? Is everything okay?" The story shows the intricacies of different phenomena of dissociation in different persons.)

Double Bind

A double bind applies to interpersonal dead-end situations. No matter what one does, it's always wrong and there's no way out. Bateson, Jackson, Haley, and Weakland developed a theory about schizophrenia incorporating this concept. What is less well known is that Bateson had his enlightening breakthrough while sitting in a tree, and that came about like this.

BATESON AND HALEY WENT TO VISIT ERICKSON. On the way from Palo Alto to Phoenix, where Erickson lived, they stopped at a national park and took a walk, all the while discussing the enigma of schizophrenic communication. They were so engrossed in their conversation that they lost track of the time, and the way. Suddenly, they found themselves face to face with a huge bear. Bateson quickly climbed a tree and Haley sought shelter in a cave. Bateson hardly had time to exhale after his climb when he saw Haley running out of the cave, almost right into the arms of the bear. Haley then turned and rushed back into the cave, only to emerge seconds later, once again almost heading into the bear. He turned around and stormed back to the cave again. Bateson called after him in despair: "Damn it, now stay put in the cave for a while!!" But Haley was on his way out again, screaming: "I can't, there's another bear in there."

Ecological Check

Ecological check is an NLP term that refers to the concept that, after a symptom-oriented effort at transformation, one should examine the level of the client's overall system, checking for reasons that might oppose this change. Perhaps the symptom fulfilled a certain purpose that ought to be taken into consideration.

The following story, which presumably dates back to an era long gone by, illustrates the importance of the ecological check.

A BABY BOY IS BORN. He is healthy and lovely. But to his parents' dismay, the child has one flaw: instead of the usual navel, he's equipped with a golden screw. The parents are anxious to correct this flaw before anyone sees it. They travel from one doctor to another and from country to country, but no one can give them any advice. Whatever they try, the screw won't budge an inch.

The child grows up, and like his parents, his main aim in life is to get rid of this screw.

He travels from one continent to another. Finally, in India, he's told that there is a tree high up in the Himalayan mountains where he will find the solution. He is given the directions and sets forth on his long and difficult journey. Sure enough, at the spot described to him stands a tree. The man with the golden belly button is very tired, and he sits down under the tree and falls asleep. He has a long dream in which he finds a bush bearing many golden tools. One of the tools is a golden wrench that seems to fit the screw in his belly button. In his dream, he takes the wrench, and he is able to untwist the screw. He wakes up under this tree in the Himalayas, somewhat dazed. He still has a vivid recollection of his dream, and he quickly pulls his shirt out of his pants and looks at his belly button: the golden screw has disappeared!

With a feeling of incomparable joy, he jumps up. Then he hears a clatter behind him. He turns around, astonished, to find that his his butt has fallen off.

EE Studies and the Psychoeducative Approach

The so-called expressed emotion (EE) studies show that with depressed and psychotic people, the probability of a relapse increases in accordance with the frequency with which negative emotions are expressed toward them (criticism, rejection, patronizing interference, etc.). The psychoeducative approach takes this into consideration and tries to instruct the relatives of such patients on how to reduce this negativity. The systemic point of view criticizes this approach on the grounds that important systemic family therapy considerations are being ignored, and especially that the index patient could become fixed in his or her role as a patient.

THE PSYCHIATRIST IS HAVING A SERIOUS TALK with the wife of a patient. Her husband is suffering from major depression. He really needs absolute rest and has to recuperate. "I know, Doctor, but he doesn't listen to me."

"Excellent," says the psychiatrist, "that's a good start."

Empirical Science

Psychotherapists are sometimes reproached for not having gathered enough empirical support for their methods. Their counterarguments often point out that even physicists have turned their backs on this scientific paradigm and have been quoted as saying: "Everything that's precise is irrelevant."

The complex problematic nature of exactitude versus relevance is revealed in the following anecdote.

TWO FRIENDS ARE HAVING A CONVERSATION: "Have you read in the paper about the recent study that says that every second German housewife is unfaithful?"

"Where does knowing about it get me? I need names, addresses, telephone numbers."

Ethnopsychiatry and Ethnomedicine

Ethnopsychiatry and ethnomedicine are areas of ethnology that deal with the medical and psychiatric knowledge of other cultures and races.

A DOCTOR INTERESTED IN ETHNOMEDICINE is traveling through Africa to find medicine men from the paleolithic period and study them. Having arrived in a capital city, he starts preparing for a trip that will take him into the heart of the country. He is sitting in a bar that evening when a tiny man who is only about 20 inches tall enters. The man is wearing the typical attire of a white farmer from this part of Africa. The bartender places the little man on the counter. The doctor is fascinated and looks at the bartender with a quizzical expression. The bartender turns to the little man and says: "Hey Joe, why don't you tell this foreigner how you called the medicine man a nasty little fraud last year!"

Extrapunitive

Jeffrey Zeig uses this category in his diagnostic model for assessing personality attributes. It describes a personality trait that reveals itself by always laying the blame on something else, never on itself.

Until a short while ago, it wasn't clear how this attitude could be explained from a family dynamics point of view. Then, while relaxing in a park, a developmental psychologist made a surprising observation on interaction that might shed some light on this problem. At the playground, he heard a mother suddenly exclaim very loudly: "Someone has shit in my kid's diaper!"

He immediately made an associative connection with Wygotski's developmental maxim: "The structure of the outer interaction becomes the structure of the inner dialogue," and developed his theory on the genesis of the extrapunitive attitude. Just how entwined such attitudes can be with the whole personality can be seen in the following episode.

A CHILD WAS ICE SKATING ON A LAKE while the mother was talking to a friend on the shore. Suddenly, a cry of dismay rang through the air. There was a hole in the ice and children were running toward the bank, screaming. A man ran in the direction of the hole, tearing off his clothes on the way, and dived into the icy water. He was gone for a few seconds, and then reappeared holding a child in his arms. With the help of two workers who just happened to pass by carrying a ladder, it was possible to drag the man, as well as the child, out of the water. The three men proudly brought the shocked child to his mother. The mother immediately turned to the man who had dived in after her child and said: "But my child was wearing a cap!"

Eye Movements: Accessing Cues

A concept of NLP claims that typical eye movements take place during processes that involve thinking and imagining. Visual imaginative processes involve other eye movements than do auditory ones, memories are accompanied by different eye movements than are newly imagined fantasies, and so on. Whoever can read these inadvertent eye movements can gain insight into the means and sequence of inner imaginative processes, and can draw conclusions as to the form of communication.

The following shows that this is ancient popular knowledge that had been lost to science temporarily, as so many things have.

A MARKETING RESEARCH GROUP IS CONDUCTING A STUDY in an agricultural area on the use of contraceptives there. The people carrying out the interviews have been carefully prepared in order to avoid embarrassing situations.

Questionnaires that can be filled out by the interviewer are also used. One of the women interviewers rings a doorbell in the middle of a village. She explains that she is conducting an inquiry in the name of the federal health agency, and would like to know whether the woman would be prepared to answer a question concerning contraceptives. The woman says that she has no problem in that respect and immediately adds that she and her husband use the bucket method. The interviewer is confused and shows the woman the questionnaire: "Is that a regional term for something that is on this list?" "No, no, those are all too expensive, not safe enough, or too unhealthy. You know, my husband is a head shorter than I am. And so he always stands on our small cleaning bucket. And then I watch very carefully. As soon as he starts to roll his eyes in a certain pattern, I kick the bucket."

Focused Attention/Awareness

The trance state that is often used during therapeutic hypnosis is a highly focused state of awareness. One is concentrating on one matter and everything else is of no importance. The faces of tennis players when serving the ball perfectly mirror this highly concentrated relaxed state.
The following situation refers to this ability, and to other things as well.

A RATHER UNIMPRESSIVE YOUNG MAN wants to join a very prestigious English country club. The admittance procedure includes a round of golf on the club's well-kept golf course. When the young man arrives for his interview, tea is being served. The club officials are surprised to see that the newcomer has brought along a field hockey stick, an ice hockey stick, and a billiard cue, but with typical British nonchalance, they let him do it his own way. They are greatly astonished, however, when the young man takes his field hockey stick, concentrates for a moment, and then demonstrates an amazing tee-off. This done, he hits the ball onto the green with his ice hockey stick and putts it into the hole from a distance of 25 feet using his billiard cue. He repeats this procedure hole after hole. After the 68th round, the slightly confused officials take him to the club bar. The young man orders a scotch and soda but insists on mixing it himself. He places the glass of soda on the bar and positions himself with his back to it. He concentrates for a minute, and then pours the scotch over his shoulder right into the glass. After this latest demonstration of his unbelievable ability to coordinate his bodily movements with such amazing precision, he is met by a barrage of questions. The young man explains that he'd always had this talent and since childhood had been training himself to perfect it. He says that after a while, however, it began to get boring, and so he had developed the habit of performing everything that had to do with bodily movements and coordination in the most difficult way possible. As a matter of principle, he plays tennis using table-tennis rackets, table tennis using badminton rackets, and so on.

"Just a moment," the club chairman interrupts him, "you say you do everything that involves bodily movements in the most difficult way possible. That leads me to a question ..."

The young man stops him: "I know what you're going to ask me. It's what everybody asks me. Well, I do that standing — in a hammock."

Forgetting About Amnesia

We say that a person has amnesia when he or she can't remember certain things. Sometimes amnesia is induced during hypnotherapy, and sometimes it occurs spontaneously.

A MAN VISITS A PSYCHIATRIST AND COMPLAINS: "My problem is that I always forget things." The psychiatrist probes further: "How long have you noticed this problem?" The patient answers, surprised: "What problem?"

Or someone says: "There are three things that I always forget: names, faces, and the third thing is uh, uh, um ..."

(Note: The amnesia joke was the first joke published in the MEG newsletter. That was the beginning.)
The following episode also sheds some light on the concept of amnesia.

OSCAR WOULD LIKE TO VISIT A BROTHEL AT LEAST ONCE IN HIS LIFE, and as he is now a widower, he decides to do it. The woman at the reception desk asks him what he is looking for and he responds: "Don't you have the most beautiful women in town?" Sure enough, after a few minutes, a very beautiful woman approaches him. She gives him a quizzical look and asks him how old he is. "I'm 94 years old," he answers. "Ninety-four," says the woman, "well you're already done with it then!" "Oh, really," he says quietly, as he reaches into his pocket with a shaking hand to get his wallet. "And how much do I owe you?"

Future Orientation

Proponents of the more recent developments in psychotherapy proclaim, with reference to Milton Erickson, that their work is solution, resource, and goal oriented. Particular attention is paid to the future as opposed to the causes and the past. (Note: One of these proponents is Steve de Shazer.)

Sometimes patients also demonstrate such positive resource orientation in front of the psychotherapist, as the following narrative shows.

AN AMERICAN WOMAN who had already undergone 743 hours of analysis decides to take a trip to Europe against the advice of her analyst, which was based on his interpretation. She remained in touch with her therapist, however, via fax and e-mail. She sent a short message from Paris: "I'm really enjoying myself immensely. Please answer at once. Why?"

During her trip to Germany, she paused in Heidelberg and came across a book by Steve de Shazer in an antiques shop. At her first analysis session upon her return home, the therapist took up where he had left off: "You are in distress because of your sexual fantasies?" She answered: "On the contrary, I'm really enjoying them."

A very good example of resource orientation is offered by the boss in the following story.

A JOB APPLICANT IS IN THE MIDDLE OF AN INTERVIEW. "Have you learned anything?" asks the boss. "No," answers the applicant. The boss: "Thank God! At least we don't have to retrain you."

(Note: I told this joke while teaching a workshop in Poland. The director of the Polish Milton Erickson Institute, Kris Klajs, intervened, saying: "This is no joke." He then described how, following the political changes of the early 1990s, a Norwegian oil company established a new chain of service stations, insisting that the staff running the stations not have worked at such stations under the old system. Obviously, it was considered easier to teach completely untrained people than to retrain old staff. Klajs also pointed out that the gas stations of the Norwegian company give the best service in the country.)

Future orientation is demonstrated in an exemplary fashion by the woman in the following anecdote.

A SUCCESSFUL BUSINESSMAN EVENTUALLY, after many years, finds the time, even if during the evening, to go to the doctor. He has been experiencing some discomfort and the complaints are increasing. But true to his motto, "A knife in the back is no reason for the likes of us to go home yet," he has stoically continued as before. The doctor examines him and pales, informing the patient that, in his medical opinion, he has only another 12 hours to live. The man returns home utterly shaken and tells the terrible news to his wife. After a few tears, they decide that his wife will prepare his favorite meal for him one last time. After that, they go to bed and make love twice. The wife falls asleep, completely exhausted, in the middle of the night. The man can't sleep. Finally, he wakes his wife and asks her to have sex with him once again, which she does. An hour later, the whole procedure is repeated, and shortly before dawn, he wakes his wife once again, saying: "Can't we do it one more time?" His wife becomes slightly irritated: "It's easy for you to talk, you don't have to get up in the morning."

Guiding Associations

Psychotherapeutic hypnosis has a lot to do with guiding associations. The following event demonstrates this process in its most subtle form.

THE WATERGATE SCANDAL IS AT ITS PEAK. Richard Nixon is desperately trying to save his neck. And to top it all off, his wife is starting to feel neglected. A friend advises her to try wearing kinky underwear. Perhaps in this way she will at least be able to attract her husband's attention. Mrs. Nixon views a display of the newest French and Italian fashions. She is especially taken with an unusual model in black silk. Extending diagonally from the panties across the stomach is a black strap that covers one breast. From there, the strap stretches across the shoulder and the back until it hooks up with the panties. The other breast is exposed. Mrs. Nixon is convinced that this model is the right one. She puts it on and lies down on their bed and waits. Long after midnight, the president wanders into the bedroom completely exhausted after endless discussions and official duties. He throws his wife an absent-minded glance, turns toward the door, and mumbles: "Oh my God, I still have to phone Moshe Dayan."

(Note: In another version of this joke, the wife lies down in black underwear and waits. The husband comes into the room, and gets a very concerned look: "Oh dear, has something happened to your mother?")

Hallucination – Positive and Negative

The professional hypnotherapist uses the term "positive hallucination" when someone hallucinates something that isn't actually there. Negative hallucination is the term used when someone just fades something out (hallucinates it away) even though, in actual fact, it is there. Negative hallucination usually arises in everyday life when awareness is rigidly focused on one part of experiencing while other aspects of the same event are faded out.

A good imagination is a precondition for hallucinating, and this ability can be applied in many ways. The following man used his highly developed hallucinating abilities so that he could become jealous more quickly. One day, his wife reproached him: "You are jealous as always." He responded: "Who is always?"

A clear example of highly focused concentration and the inherent negative hallucination can be seen in this police report. The officer was supposed to investigate a suspected case of insurance fraud.

Officer: "How do you explain the fact that the burglar was able to clean out the whole apartment even though you were there all the time?"
Victim: "That must have been because the scoundrel left the TV set behind."

The following example illustrates the importance of hallucinatory phenomena in family life.

Wife: "If you don't stop playing the saxophone, I'll go crazy."
Husband: "You already are. I stopped playing an hour ago."

Whether the hallucinatory phenomena in the following story are of a negative or positive nature has been a subject of controversy among hypnosis professionals for many years.

A DISTINGUISHED-LOOKING ENGLISHMAN in pinstripes and bowler hat is calmly standing in Trafalgar Square in the middle of the rush hour, holding the evening paper before him. A bobby approaches him, clearing his throat. The man is so engrossed in the *Times* that the bobby's efforts to attract his attention go unheeded. The bobby's attempts to draw the man back into reality become a bit bolder. He lightly taps the man on the arm: "Excuse me, Sir, your fly is open and your penis is showing."

The man stretches his arms and holds the paper slightly away from him, glances down the length of his own body, and says in a surprised tone of voice: "Oh, she's gone?"

> *(Note: I recently found a variation of this joke. In London's Hyde Park, a young man is exercising, doing push-ups. An old man approaches him and says: "Sir, you can stop, now. The lady seems to have gone.")*

Helper Personality

A helper personality has taken the dictum "It is more blessed to give than to receive" so much to heart that it gives to others in an almost merciless egotism without giving the others the chance to establish their own steps in the blessed direction.

The following story shows how someone — presumably a retired psychotherapist — has achieved a slightly more detached and balanced attitude toward the need to help, and yet, despite outward detachment, hasn't given it up completely:

Two fierce-looking men are lowering a man who has been bound and gagged onto the railway tracks. An old woman watches them with interest, and eventually says: "It's no concern of mine, but these tracks have been out of use for seven years."

(Note: In a variation of this joke, two members of the IRA in Ireland are lowering a bound and gagged man to the railway tracks. A couple watches from the window of a nearby house. The wife says to her husband: "If I were interested in politics, I would go down and tell them that those tracks are no longer in use.")

Homeostasis

Translated, homeostasis could mean "coming to a standstill on the same level." This term is used in family therapy to describe the pathological effort families make to stay the way they are and accept no changes even though outside demands make changes neccessary.

The following story graphically demonstrates this tenacity, yet still shows how one can induce changes by applying skillful interventions.

A FATHER, MOTHER, AND THEIR 17-YEAR-OLD DAUGHTER have gathered for a festive meal at home. After the meal, a quarrel develops around the subject of who has to clear the table and wash the dishes. The mother says that she did the cooking, and the father emphasizes how hard he had to work all week to feed his family. The daughter is furious because it all seems to boil down to her again. The fight escalates and the daughter lies down on the floor in protest, underlining her decision not to clean up no matter what. The mother lies down next to her so that no one can doubt her resolve not to do it either. Eventually, the father lies down next to them as well. They decide that the first person to move is the one who will do the washing up. The minutes go by. (What we see here is homeostasis at work — a complete standstill on the same level.) At the same time, on a nearby road, a driver is having trouble with his car. He thinks it might be the starter. In search of a hammer, he approaches the house of the quarreling family. He rings the doorbell. Nothing moves. He rings once more, still no reaction. The house seems inhabited and he sees that the door to the porch is open. He calls, but nobody answers. As this is the only house in the vicinity, he enters and looks for a hammer. He searches the house and nobody interrupts. Finally, he finds a hammer. On his way back to the door, he catches a glimpse of the dining room and stiffens. He sees the three people lying on the floor, motionless. It takes a few seconds for him to regain his composure. Then the attractiveness of the daughter engages his attention. So, without further ado, he lies down and has sex with her. And nobody moves.

Carrying the hammer, the man goes back to his car. He gives the starter a few energetic blows without success. "Maybe it's the spark plugs then," he thinks. He decides to return to the house to look for a spark plug key in the father's well-equipped workshop. For decency's sake, he rings the doorbell again and calls out. Still nobody moves. He rummages around and finds what he is looking for. On his way out, he glances at the motionless mother and he thinks: "Damn it, she's even more attractive than her daughter." He lies down and has sex with her. Back at his car, he removes the spark plugs, cleans them, and puts them back in place. Still the car won't start. A bit at a loss, he examines the engine and discovers a bare wire. "Insulating tape" immediately comes to mind. Once again, he goes back to the house. He gives the doorbell a quick ring and enters the house to look for insulating tape. On leaving, he passes the dining room again, when suddenly the father jumps up and calls out: "OK, OK, I'll wash the dishes."

Hypnosystemic Family Therapy

As the name implies, hypnosystemic family therapy is a combination of Ericksonian hypnotherapy and systemic therapy.

According to certain sources that are usually very well informed, the following case seems to have played a part in the development of this approach.

GUNTHER SCHMIDT, one of the main proponents of this technique, gives the participants in a beginners' workshop a break for lunch. A client is waiting in the corridor. The man describes his problems. It seems that his sexual desire has disappeared entirely and only hypnosis can help him.

After obtaining the necessary details, Schmidt starts the trance induction and the hypnotic intervention: "You are lying on a couch and are completely relaxed. Fully relaxed and wonderfully calm, you are listening to your favorite music. There's a fire crackling in the fireplace. You haven't seen a woman in five years. For the last five years, you haven't seen a woman. Your longing becomes greater and greater. You can smell the fire in the fireplace and you are listening to the lovely music. The door opens softly and your longing becomes immense. A beautiful woman enters. She is only lightly clad and you can smell her perfume and the fragrance of her hair. An irresistible passion overwhelms you. Your body is trembling slightly. And while your body is shivering and trembling, you slowly start talking and describe what you are experiencing..."

Schmidt pauses for a moment to discreetly enable the client to tell the story according to his own inner fantasies. And believe it or not, after only a short delay, the client starts talking while his body is still trembling. He softly repeats one sentence over and over again: "And what would Mommy say to this? And what would Mommy say to this?"

Even before the workshop participants had returned from their luncheon break, Schmidt had acquired some important insights regarding the necessary combination of hypnotic and systemic methods. And it is said that since that moment of scientific creativity, he has retained the habit of seeing clients during his workshop breaks.

(Note: Gunther Schmidt is a popular family therapist in Germany, as well as the vice president of the German Milton Erickson Society. He is known for his frenetic

working style. One training group will be waiting for Schmidt at 9 a.m., just as he is ending a family therapy session. When the training group breaks for lunch at 12 p.m., another family is already waiting for him. And when the workshop ends at 6 p.m., yet another family is waiting for Schmidt.)

Hypnotic Speech Rhythms

Trance inductions can be based on the use of certain rhythms. Some use the rhythm of drums, others use rhythmics of speech.

On a State visit to Egypt, Helmut Kohl asks to be relieved of his bodyguards and be allowed to take a walk in the desert. With great misgivings, the Egyptian officials finally grant his request. The security guards thoroughly search and secure the area. But both the German and Egyptian guards fail to notice a pack of lions roaming there.

So Kohl is taking his solitary walk through the desert, admiring the landscape, when he rounds a huge sand dune and is suddenly confronted by a lion, which crouches down, ready to spring. Kohl recalls his rhetoric abilities and slowly starts talking to the lion. The lion calms down and begins to feel sleepier and sleepier. He sways his head from side to side, lies down, closes his eyelids, and sinks into a deep sleep. Kohl wants to retreat, but then the lioness comes around the dune. She sees her partner lying on the floor motionless, crouches, and whips her tail to and fro. Kohl starts talking to her in a quiet manner, and lo and behold, the lioness also lies down and goes into a semiconscious state. Kohl manages to do the same with the lion's brother. Just as Kohl commences his final retreat, the father of the lion appears. Kohl starts talking to him quietly in well-measured tones, but the old lion just continues his approach, and knocks Kohl to the ground with one stroke of his huge paw.

Two small monkeys are sitting high in a palm tree, watching. One turns to the other and says: "Didn't I tell you the babbling down there would stop as soon as the old deaf one got here?"

Implications

The term "implications" in connection with suggestions is used when something is being said without its being said outright. When someone asks, "Do you still beat your wife?" the question may be focused on the "still," but the implication is that the person beat his wife in the past.
  Milton Erickson once told the following story.

A COWBOY GETS MARRIED. After the ceremony, he lets his wife mount the horse on which he is sitting and together they ride to his new log cabin. After a while, the horse stumbles and the cowboy says softly: "One." They ride on, the horse stumbles again, and the cowboy softly says: "Two." Shortly before reaching the log cabin, the horse stumbles for the third time. The cowboy stops the horse, lets his wife dismount, then gets off himself, and shoots it. His bride shouts at him: "Are you crazy? You shot the horse just because it stumbled?" The cowboy answers softly: "One."
  And ever since that day, his wife thinks back wistfully to the time, long before the wedding, when her husband-to-be asked her: "Should we take the shortcut through the forest, or are you in a hurry today?"

Individuation – Related

Related Individuation, a concept developed by Helm Stierlin, is based on the two extremes of over- and underindividuation. Overindividuation applies to a lack of contact and relationships with others. The individual is too isolated. Underindividuation, on the other hand, implies a lack of boundaries; symbiotic structures are predominant. Related individuation means that these two poles have been reconciled: greater individuation, where everyone can stand on his or her own two feet, goes hand in hand with a more intense relationship.

The following dialogue provides an ideal example.

Farmer's wife: "Lena is having a baby."
Farmer: "Ah well, that's her problem."
Farmer's wife: "She says it's yours."
Farmer: "That's my problem."
Farmer's wife: "And what am I to do now?"
Farmer: "That's your problem."

The problem of reconciling one's own individual interests with being tied up in relationships and obligations can be found recurring throughout the history of humankind.

It's also obvious in this event that took place a long time ago and has been deleted from the Gospels.

AT THE LAST SUPPER, the waiter asked: "All together?" Judas replied: "No, separate checks please!"

The following game of bridge also sheds some light on this subject.

THE WOMEN ARE TALKING ABOUT THEIR HUSBANDS and their relationships. One woman asks her partner: "Have you ever gone on vacation separately?"

The other woman confirms having done so two years earlier.
"And? Did you enjoy doing it?"
"Yes, very much."

"And your husband?"
"I really can't say. He hasn't come back yet."

> *A disturbance in the relationship between symbiosis and individuation is assumed to play a part with families where at least one schizophrenic member is involved. Sometimes aphorisms afford an insight into this field of tension. One can find them on building walls, in public toilets, and in subways, to name just a few places. A small excerpt should motivate the psychotherapeutically schooled readers to keep their eyes open and seek out these places the next time they decide to travel or take a walk. I haven't a clue as to whether such profound thoughts can also be found in the women's public lavatories, but I've discovered some really relevant statements on a number of subjects in the men's toilets.*

ON THIS SUBJECT OF "related individuation," I came across the following aphorisms: "Rather schizophrenic than completely alone," and "Stop thinking about me all the time. I want to be alone once in a while."

> *(Note: Question: "What is the difference between intercourse and masturbation?" Answer: "With intercourse, you make contact with more people.")*

The Inner Voice

A few psychotherapeutic methods emphasize the importance of listening to one's inner voice: "Trust your unconscious," "Trust your intuition," or the like.

The following story offers a glimpse of the possibilities that can arise when listening to one's inner voice.

A GAMBLER WHO HAS RUN OUT OF LUCK and has already resorted to all the systems he can find is once again playing roulette. He laments about his bad luck to another player. As it happens, the other player is a psychotherapist who is seeking to understand the addiction to gambling suffered by some of his clients by trying it himself.

The therapist advises the luckless player: "You must heed your inner voice." The player isn't sure what the therapist means by this but the idea intrigues him, and it stays in his mind.

Some days later, the gambler returns to the casino. While trying his luck at the roulette table, he suddenly hears someone say: "Place your bet on 32!" Astonished, he gazes about him, but there's nobody there. He doesn't realize that it was his inner voice speaking. Nevertheless, he decides to bet on 32, and the number wins. The croupier calls the next round and the man hears the voice say: "All on 3." And 3 wins. The voice goes on: "Now all on 32." The man is doubtful, didn't 32 win just a short while earlier? The professional players are gradually gathering around the table. And once again the voice: "Place everything on 32!" The man pushes his large stack of chips toward 32 and the little ball starts spinning. It comes to rest tentatively on 32, but then, with a final spin, it settles into the compartment next to it. The voice says: "Oh shit!"

Intervention

Intervention is a common term describing a particular psychotherapeutic maneuver. An alternative expression is "the therapeutic lever," which needs to be applied at the right spot.

To some, these terms sound too mechanistic; others find them too presumptuous. And yet, knowing when and how the therapeutic lever should be applied can be of great significance in the solving of problems.

The following story from Isaac Asimov provides an impressive example.

A YOUNG MAN COMES HOME ON VACATION after having spent a few months away as an apprentice in a distant town. The family is eager to hear how he is enjoying his apprenticeship. His parents were worried that working in a funeral parlor might not be the right job for him, and are very relieved when their son starts talking enthusiastically about the funeral director and about his education there. He explains that the job is very important and involves a lot of things that need to be learned. His boss, for instance, is a true master in handling the delicate situations that often arise when arranging a funeral. The family is curious about this, and the son offers an example.

"Recently, we had a very special case. The good names and reputations of two families were at stake, as was the reputation of a renowned hotel.

"A son of one of the families and a daughter of the other family fell deeply in love. Their families, however, were staunchly opposed to their marrying because a feud had been raging between the families for generations. Despondent, the two young people went to the famous hotel, checked into a very expensive room, and committed suicide. So here they were, lying dead in the room, and it would be our task to deliver the bodies to their respective families without making the story of the suicides public and ruining the hotel's reputation. The director put on his best black frock coat, his white gloves, and his expensive homburg, and picked up his lacquered black cane, the one with the ivory knob. Then he asked me to accompany him. I was very pleased at this show of confidence in me.

"We went into the hotel, took the elevator upstairs, and found the room with the number that had been given to us. With some reluctance, we quietly entered the room. But how shall I describe the scene that met our eyes? These two beautiful people were lying on the bed almost completely naked. They were locked in a tight embrace. Their lips were slightly open as if they had been about to say something. It was a picture that almost moved even my experienced boss to tears. There was only one problem."

The family hung on every word and called out, almost in unison: "What kind of problem?"

The young man continued: "They were clasping each other so tightly that I, personally, couldn't see any other way to separate them, except by force. Carrying them away together seemed just as difficult. I could almost see the cogs working in my boss' brain, and suddenly his face lit up. With his experience and ingenuity, he seemed to have found an answer. He took his cane in his hand, speculatively weighing it for a moment. Then, with remarkable dexterity, he delivered a light blow at the right angle between the two bodies and they fell apart with a sudden movement and a somewhat strange sound."

The son paused and took a deep breath. Excitedly, the father asked him: "And that solved the problem then, didn't it?"

"Well," said the son, "not quite. As it turned out, we were in the wrong room."

Intuition and Observation

Old masters of psychotherapy and speech therapy, such as Milton Erickson and Charles Van Riper, were said to possess legendary intuitive abilities. Some people attributed it to extrasensory perception. Erickson always rejected this view, and pointed out that his was a highly trained ability to observe. Both Erickson and Van Riper were able to fool fortune tellers with their abilities.

This subtle interplay — you might even call it a fine line between the ability to observe and intuition — is exemplified by the following story.

Two men who haven't seen each other for quite a while meet at an official reception. After a short conversation, one says to the other: "I can't understand how you can wear such vulgar red underwear to such a festive occasion." The second man is visibly shocked: "How do you know that?" "Well," answers the other, "first of all, by intuition! And second, you forgot to put on your trousers."

It is a well-known fact that the famous fictional detective Sherlock Holmes was also a master of the art of observation and intuition. One day, Sir Arthur Conan Doyle, Holmes' creator, got off the train in Paris and hailed a taxi. The taxi driver asked: "Where to, Mr. Doyle?" Conan Doyle looked very surprised: "You know me?" The taxi driver answered: "Not really. I know your books, but I've never seen your picture." "But then how did you know me? How do you know who I am?"

"Well, I read in the paper that you were vacationing in the south of France. And then I noticed that you came from the platform of the train that arrived from Marseilles. You are sporting the color of about ten days in the sun. Furthermore, there is an ink spot on your finger and that points in the direction of your being an author. Moreover, you are dressed like an Englishman. All that combined seemed to make it obvious that you are Conan Doyle, the creator of Sherlock Holmes." Impressed, Conan Doyle said enthusiastically: "But you are a Sherlock Holmes yourself! The way you pieced all those little observations together..." The driver interrupted him: "There is one other small detail though that helped. There is a name tag on your suitcase."

Inward Orientation

Trance induction often includes an inward orientation. Perhaps this signifies a relaxed utilization of an old phenomenon. Over millions of years of evolutionary history, retreating into oneself in times of danger, or, for example, when facing death, has proved to be a very useful ability. "To turn tail" would be a vernacular description of this phenomenon.

AMERICAN FOOTBALL IS A TOUGH SPORT that reminds one of the combats of the good old days. Miller is a highly paid substitute on a professional team. Game after game finds him sitting on the sidelines, hoping to join in the game, but the coach doesn't call on him. The season is coming to an end. Miller has a very important private appointment at exactly the same time as a critical home game is scheduled. He is in a tight spot and eventually manages to persuade his wife to take his place on the bench. "You know," he says, "not once during the season have I been used as a replacement, and considering how important this game is, the chances of my being called on are pretty slim. You'll go to the stadium wearing a helmet and my padded uniform with my number, and nobody will recognize you." In spite of her doubts, Mrs. Miller agrees to do it.

The game begins and Miller (supposedly) as usual is sitting on the substitute bench. The opposing team is an extremely unfair adversary and one player after the other is carried off the field injured. Toward the end of the game, Miller's time comes. He is the only player left on the bench, and the coach needs him as a replacement. Mrs. Miller storms onto the field with the courage born of despair and immediately is seriously fouled. She blacks out and is carried off the field. She comes to as the club's masseur, who is busily massaging her genital area, says reassuringly: "Please don't get upset, Miller. Please remain calm! Once we've got hold of the testicles, the penis will surely follow as well."

The Language of the Unconscious

Milton Erickson was a master in perceiving messages from the unconscious implicit in the words chosen by his clients. He often said that therapists should be able to understand and speak the clients' languages. The German author Arno Schmidt describes this process regarding the language used by Karl May in his book Sitara. *(Note: Karl May wrote some 70 books of fiction about Native Americans around 100 years ago on such subjects as the wars between the tribes and the friendship between an Indian chief and a German hero. Almost everyone in Germany is familiar with his books.) As an example, Schmidt points out that Karl May often combines the words "Wald" (woods) and "Heim" (home) in various ways, such as "unheimlicher Wald" (sinister woods). For Schmidt, there seems to be an unconscious connection between the use of these word combinations and the time May spent in the Waldheim Penitentiary.*

The following therapeutic episode could prove interesting to an expert on unconscious language (verbalization).

THE PATIENT TELLS HER ANALYST about all that has happened since their last session: "I bought rabbits and prepared one for my husband's dinner each day." The analyst — his operational strategy definitely contains a systemic component — asks: "And what does your husband have to say to this?" The patient answers: "Nothing. Not one word. Not one single word. All he does is stare at me. With his big red eyes."

As I said, Milton Erickson was a master at perceiving such subliminal overtones in a conveyed message and then using them therapeutically.

SOME OF MILTON ERICKSON'S FOLLOWERS felt obliged to learn and practice this complex process. One of these students came from Germany and traveled to Phoenix to attend an international convention. In the hotel elevator, he encountered a beautiful Mexican woman. As luck would have it, she spoke neither English nor German and he spoke not a word of Spanish. Quick as lightning, he took out his notebook and sketched the outlines of a taxi. The woman smiled at him and nodded. So, on the spur of the moment, they hailed a taxi and drove through town. He took his pad and drew a restaurant with tables and dinner plates. She nodded and he ordered the taxi driver to take them to a restaurant that, according to the sightseeing tips included in his convention packet, was the best and most expensive in Phoenix. They had a splendid dinner. The mood was amiable. Then he drew a picture of a couple dancing closely and was rewarded by the lovely woman's bright smile and nod indicating her consent. She accompanied him to a club, and, after a couple of dances, she took his notebook and drew an awkward, but recognizable, picture of a big four-poster bed. After he had escorted her to her door and given her a parting kiss, he couldn't help but stand there a moment in wonderment. He was still speculating on his way back to the convention and during the convention itself. He continued deliberating on the plane journey back home. He felt a bit frustrated, and even inadequate. How on earth was it possible? What nonverbal minimal cues had enabled this young woman to deduce that he had once worked for a furniture store during his college vacation?

Learned Helplessness

Learned helplessness is one of the concepts with which one tries to explain the development of depression. (Note: The concept of learned helplessness was introduced to the field of psychology by Martin Seligman.)

If, for example, a human being, or an animal, is exposed to a situation that always ends in a negative way, no matter what the person or animal tries to do (e.g., an animal is "rewarded" with a surge of current applied at random, no matter how cleverly and resourcefully it behaves), this will eventually lead to resignation and apathy, as the following story shows.

A STUTTERER IS SITTING ON A BUS and asks the man sharing his seat: "Coucoucould yoyoyoyou tttttttttell mmmmmme, whwhwhwhwen wwwwwe've arararararrrrrrived at thththththe ssssssssssstation. The other passenger doesn't move and just sits there, completely apathetic and motionless. The stutterer tries again: "Ppppplease tttttttell mmmmmmme whwhwhwhen wwwwwe've arrrrrived at tthththththe ssssssssttation." Once again he gets no reaction. A woman across the aisle intervenes and says: "I'll tell you when we've arrived at the station." On leaving the bus, the stutterer slaps the uncooperative passenger. The woman comments: "That serves you right." The man answers: "I wowwowoould hhhhhhhave gggggggot one on thththththe kkkkkkisser ininin aaaaany ccccase."

Loyalty

Loyalty is a central concept in the contextual family therapy developed by Ivan Boszormenyi-Nagy. It implies how certain attitudes and behavioral patterns can be passed down in a family from generation to generation. Loyalty explains, for example, why and how, from one generation to the next, the oldest child always takes over the family restaurant.

The following story features this mechanism.

THE SUMMER OLYMPICS: In the stadium where the track and field events are held, the discipline of throwing the hammer is underway and has entered its final stage. The last round begins. The American, currently in third place, enters the ring, concentrates, and throws the hammer. Loud cheering accompanies the flight of the hammer for a new Olympic record: he is now leading the field and will probably win the gold medal.

The reporters follow the beaming American and the TV station, which holds exclusive rights to all games taking place inside the stadium, requests an interview when he arrives at the edge of the cinder track. The reporter asks him excitedly: "What gave you the strength of body and mind to improve your performance so unbelievably during the final round?" The athlete answers: "Well, my father was a lumberjack and my grandfather before him was a lumberjack. You start off with a lot of strength in your arms, and working in the woods gives you the peace and quiet you need." The reporter interrupts him because the Russian, currently in second place, has entered the ring. The Russian takes a moment to concentrate, executes his four legendary pirouettes, and sends the hammer flying. The spectators cry out. The hammer hits the ground just a few inches away from the world record mark, yet still clearly beyond it. The stadium goes crazy. The reporter grabs the Russian athlete and breathlessly says: "This is unbelievable! This must mean the gold medal! Where did you get the strength of body and mind for this counterattack after the American's new Olympic record?"

The Russian answers: "Oh, that's easy. My father is a miner, my grandfather before him was a miner. Right from the beginning, you possess the necessary strength of body and mind, even in difficult situations."

The stadium becomes quiet. The German athlete enters the ring. It's the last throw in the competition and he had been leading until now. He concentrates and completes three vigorous and coordinated turns. The hammer flies further and further as the ever-louder cheers of the audience become a roar. It's the most extraordinary world record of the century. The athlete leaps into the air as the fans wildly applaud his tremendous feat. The reporter has a difficult time dragging the German away from the adulation. When he finally gets him to face the camera, he asks him the same question: "Tell me, where did you get the strength of body and mind that enabled you to deliver such a fabulous throw and win the gold medal after the unbelievable performances of the American and Russian athletes?" The German athlete answers: "That wasn't so difficult. My father was a ne'er-do-well and my grandfather before him was a ne'er-do-well. And early in my life, my grandfather told me: 'Lad, if anyone ever puts a hammer in your hands, make sure to throw it as far away from you as you possibly can.' "

Mediating

Mediation is an attempt by a counselor to intervene between two people who are at odds with each other.

The father of a family suffers from heart disease and succumbs after a long illness. He has failed to settle his affairs and to clearly name his beneficiaries. His children are engaged in a bitter fight at the probate court. The judge makes a few proposals concerning amicable agreements, but to no avail. Finally, the court engages a mediator. The various parties retire for deliberation with their respective lawyers and the mediator. After much consideration and debate, the lawyers reappear: "We've reached a partial settlement. The deceased's pacemaker goes to the Red Cross."

Meditation

According to the magazine Psychology Today, meditation may be identical to what we used to call dozing. In the end, we know very little about the nature of different modes of consciousness, and that must have been how this woman felt.

Two mothers are talking about their adult sons. One says: "Recently, my son started meditating. I don't know what it is, but it's definitely better than sitting around doing nothing."

Meeting Clients in Their Own Frames of Reference

Meeting clients in their own frames of reference is one of the demands that psychotherapists schooled in the Ericksonian method of thinking make on themselves. The client's view of life should be respected and utilized. This principle is also being given increasing attention outside of therapy since, by applying it, resistance can be avoided and better contact established. Less well known is the fact that a division of the police, GFE 9, has undergone special training incorporating these ideas. (Note: GFE refers to a training program of the German Milton Erickson Society in which social workers, nurses, teachers, and the like learn better communication skills, that is, to utilize metaphors, to be sensitive, to use helpful suggestions, and to avoid suggestions with negative implications. GSG 9 is an elite troop of German police with special antiterrorist training. It was this unit that successfully ended the hijacking of a Lufthansa jet in Mogadischu, Africa, in the 1970s.)

During a supervisory patrol, we were able to confirm the high standards to which the GFE officers have conformed in implementing this principle. Following is the report issued by the supervisor.

SOME POLICE OFFICERS wear small buttons in their lapels declaring: "GFE 9. In merciless kindness — your friend and helper." (Note: "The police, your friend and helper" was often used by the German police in public relations material. To the German public in the 1950s and 1960s, the police still bore the negative reputation acquired during Hitler's regime, and the department wanted to establish a new image — that of a helper and friend of the people rather than an institution to be feared.)

A PEDESTRIAN ASKS ONE OF TWO OFFICERS: "Is one allowed to cross the road when the traffic light is orange?"

The officer answers: "No, on neither orange nor raspberry, but only when it shows parsley."

SOON AFTERWARD, the special branch officers receive a message on the police radio ordering them to a store that sells household articles. The salesperson is in despair: "This gentleman insists on buying a Volkswagen here."

The GFE officer spontaneously establishes a good rapport with the customer by asking: "Would you like to have it wrapped or would you rather eat it now?"

A SHORT TIME LATER, the two officers stop an obviously drunk driver who has been racing through the streets like a lunatic. "What do you think you're doing?" "I'm taking part in an important rally and am momentarily in the lead!" the racing driver complains. "Oh," says the GFE officer, "I have to submit you to a drug test."

Later that evening, the two officers are checking out a shady bar. The atmosphere is a bit tense and the officers don't seem to be too popular. The bartender is looking for an opportunity to provoke the men and show them up in public. One officer orders a beer. "Two sixty," says the bartender. The officer hands him a five dollar bill. The bartender dips his hand into the cash register in a provokingly casual manner, extracts 24 dimes, and throws them on the floor next to the police officer. A guest who has been leaning against the bar in a provokingly casual manner starts laughing. Then silence reigns for a while. The police officer takes a sip from his glass, puts it down, reaches into his jacket pocket in a provokingly casual manner, takes out two dimes, and throws them on the floor, saying: "One more beer, please, for the gentleman with the hearty laugh."

THE OFFICERS ARE SATISFIED with the events of the day and with their special training. "Do you remember how confused we used to be?" says one. "Yes," answers the other one, laughing, "I remember my helplessness when a man came into the station house between Frankfurt and Heidelberg and asked me how to get to Stuttgart. I asked the driver: 'Do you want to travel via Heidelberg or via Karlsruhe?' And he answered: 'Actually, I want to travel via car.'"

ONE OFFICER MENTIONS THAT HIS GIRLFRIEND is interested in his special training. She is a public prosecutor. A short while earlier, an exhibitionist had managed to undress during court proceedings before anyone could intervene. She just gave him a cursory glance and asked that the case be dismissed on the grounds of insignificant findings.

> *It must be added here that the new training group is making progress. During an intermediate exam, one of the officers was asked: "Let's assume you are on a special mission in Swabia and have received orders to disperse a crowd. How would you go about it?" The officer answered: "I would give my troops the order 'Hats off!' and send them out to take up a collection."*
>
> *It is said that the Swabian people are very frugal. The joke is that the Scots were forced to leave Swabia many generations ago because they wasted too much money.*

Metaphoric Communication

The use of stories and metaphors for change is found in almost every human culture. Modern psychotherapy also utilizes stories in many ways. Family therapy, for example, as well as hypnotherapy, tries to identify the client's images and metaphors and change them.

The techniques of storytelling and using metaphors traditionally have been used by clerics of various religions.

AN 85-YEAR-OLD JEWISH MAN marries a 25-year-old woman. Six months later, the woman is pregnant. The man seeks out a rabbi to ask for advice: "Rabbi, what do you think? Can the child be mine?"

The rabbi replies: "To answer that, I have to tell you a story. An eldery English gentleman loves big-game hunting and he books a trip to Africa, where he goes on a safari. One morning, he wakes up early and tramps through the jungle. When he gets to the middle of the jungle, he notices that instead of his gun, he has taken along his umbrella. He doesn't have much time to philosophize over his forgetfulness, as suddenly a lion appears in front of him, swishing its tail nervously. In a reflex action, the elderly gentleman grabs his umbrella and takes aim. A shot is heard and the lion sinks to the ground, dead."

The rabbi is silent and looks the 85-year-old man straight in the eye. The man looks puzzled, and he finally says: "But how can that be? Someone else must have delivered the shot." The rabbi says: "That's exactly how I see it."

Another story, also from Africa, shows how a Christian missionary used metaphors and parables.

THE MISSIONARY HAS BEEN WORKING with this particular tribe for five years. The chief's wife gives birth to her third child. The child, however, has a conspicuously light complexion. The chief calls the missionary to him and begins: "Missionary, look around you. As far as I can see, and as far as you can see, there are black people everywhere. The only white in the area is you. Now, my wife's child is white. What is your opinion about that?"

The missionary starts perspiring. Experienced as he is, he searches for a parable. "Chief," he begins, "Chief, over there on the slope I see our herd of sheep. As far as I can see, all the sheep are white. And yet, one single lamb is black." The chief looks nervously at the missionary: "OK, OK. I won't tell if you won't tell."

Sometimes, psychotherapists marry each other and use metaphorical techniques to structure their own love lives.

WEDDING NIGHT: He admires her beauty and becomes poetic: "This mountainous range! This valley! This charming meadow! . . ." After a while, he falls asleep. This continues for the next four nights. Finally, his wife wakes him in the middle of the night and says: "If there isn't a tree in this meadow very soon, it will be sold!"

A TRUCK STOP: It is late afternoon. Joe sits at a table and has the waitress bring him 12 hard-boiled eggs. His old friend, Charlie, shows up unexpectedly. Shaking his head in disbelief, Charlie asks: "Twelve hard-boiled eggs. Isn't that a bit much?" Joe answers: "First, it's none of your business. Second, I like hard-boiled eggs. And third, they bring real ink to the pen."

Joe goes to the men's room and when he comes back, he sees that Charlie also has ordered 12 hard-boiled eggs and is throwing them out of the window, one after the other. Joe: "What the hell are you doing?" Charlie: "First, it is none of your business. Second, I do not like hard-boiled eggs. And third, I have nobody to write to at the moment."

Minimal Cues,
and How to Read Them

Milton Erickson was known for his ability to draw conclusions concerning the well-being of a client from minimal, nonverbal cues.

Sometimes he recited stories and watched for these minimal cues. Such cues could include a change in the breathing pattern, facial reactions, slight movements of the body, and the like, which would validate his diagnoses and therapeutic appraisals.

The following story demonstrates this approach.

THE HEAD OF A LARGE JEWISH FAMILY sees his rabbi and complains about the lack of a sense of morality these days. He had purchased a very nice new umbrella and now it has been stolen. He tells the rabbi that the worst part is that the thief must have been a member of his own family. "You can't even trust your own relatives," he adds. He explains that he suspects one of two relatives in particular. "It must have been one of them. But which one?" He doesn't want to take the risk of accusing the wrong one.

The rabbi answers: "It's really quite simple. You are the head of the family. You shall gather your family around you on the Sabbath. You will decorate the table with some candles. And then you will begin to pray and sing. While you're doing this, you will quite nonchalantly pick up the Bible and start to recite a few lines from it. A bit of this, a bit of that, and, quite by chance, you will come to passages by Moses and start reading a few lines here and a few lines there. And again, quite accidentally, you will happen upon the Ten Commandments. You slowly recite one Commandment after the other. When you reach the Commandment "Thou shalt not steal," you read this with slightly more emphasis, then pause, while observing the others out of the corner of your eye. Does anyone become restless or start blushing? If so, you will know who the culprit was."

The man is enthusiastic about this advice, and, promising to keep the rabbi informed, hurries home. Two weeks later, the man returns to the rabbi, carrying his wonderful umbrella. He recounts what happened: "It was great! Everything worked out the way you said it would: I summoned the family to come and I decorated the table with a few candles. First, I prayed and sang with them. Then I fetched the Bible and started reading from it. I read a bit of this and a bit of that. Then, quite by accident, I opened the Book of Moses and read a few lines here and a few lines there. Then, quite by chance as it seemed, I started to read the Ten Commandments, one after the other. And just in the middle of reading 'Thou shalt not commit adultery' — right at that moment — I remembered where I'd forgotten my umbrella.''

> *(Note: Many years ago, in my workshops, I sometimes would look around after delivering the punch line: "Thou shalt not commit adultery." But for some participants, this was too intensive a demonstration of the technique of "diagnosing via minimal cues.")*

Model Learning

Model learning is a concept from the theory of learning: "Education is useless. Children learn from role models." As far as I can recall, this was said by a famous pedagog and philosopher whose name I seem to have forgotten (see amnesia).

The following story shows just what a role model with the ability to sweep you along can do.

PLACE: A hotel bar on the 50th floor of an old building. It's quite late. A few men are there who have been drinking heavily. The bragging and the jokes are getting bolder by the minute. Finally, one of the men claims that soon he will open the window, jump out, disappear, then reappear and continue drinking as if nothing has happened. The others roar with laughter. Before they can react, the show-off yanks open the window and jumps. Sober dismay. After a few seconds, he really reappears. His drinking companions think they must have been dreaming (see hallucinations). The braggard mumbles thickly: "Want me to show you again?" He jumps out of the window once more and reappears again shortly afterward. The drunkest of the group rouses himself: "Aaanythhing you cccan do, I can do betteeeeeeeer!" Before the others realize what's happening, he dives out of the window. There's a long drawn-out scream and he hits the pavement below.

Says the bartender: "I hate to say this, Batman, but you're sure a mean asshole when you're drunk."

Monoideism

The Englishman Charles Braid introduced the term "hypnosis." However, he wanted to change it to "monoideism" later on, after he recognized that hypnos — which means sleep — doesn't do the nature of a trance state any credit. He found monoideism (one-ideaism) more suitable, as it describes the circumstances in a more appropriate way, namely, that the person in trance is focused on one thing only and screens out everything else that is happening and is not important.

Many people manage to do this at breakfast, without a formal trance induction, by stirring their cups and stirring and stirring until there's nothing left to stir when what they're actually doing is stirring around in their day's work or in the dreams they had the night before. The more advanced of the breakfast monoideists usually feel a painful stinging in one eye, which is attributable to the fact that they forgot to remove the spoon from their cup before drinking.

A MAN HAS BEEN PRACTICING GOLF with his teacher for quite a long time. Now he may finally set out alone with only his caddy accompanying him. Meanwhile, the golf teacher is sitting in the clubhouse, reading the latest golf magazines.

After about half an hour, his pupil returns, very upset. "Imagine what happened to me. I tee off at the first hole. The ball sails through the air toward the street, right into the eye of the driver of a convertible. The car swerves from left to right and the driver loses control of his vehicle. It overturns, slides down a slope, and comes to a stop right in the middle of the railroad tracks. The express train can't stop in time and derails. There is chaos, there probably are lot of casualties. What am I supposed to do?" The teacher answers: "Like I've always told you: keep your legs together when hitting the ball."

It's a few years later and our golfer friend has finally found the correct, focused attitude toward his game.

He's sitting in the clubhouse when another member approaches him. "From what I've heard, you've experienced another great tragedy." The golfer lifts his glass and takes a sip of beer while his eyes cloud over. He says haltingly: "You mean the business with Egan? We were in the middle of a game when, at the ninth hole, he suddenly collapsed. He was dead. Just simply dead." The other responds: "I heard you carried him back to the clubhouse. That must have been damned difficult. He must have weighed at least 200 pounds!"

Our golfer answers: "Well you're right, only the really difficult part wasn't the carrying, but the putting him down before every stroke and then picking him up again."

Multiple-Level Communication

So-called multiple-level communication is a characteristic of Ericksonian hypnotherapy. It means that something that's been said can have several different meanings on different levels. This triggers search processes and confusion, but also sudden understanding.

Simple forms of multilevel communication include only one double meaning. Example: "I went to the internal revenue office yesterday! I really gave them the business." It is more blessed to give than to receive (Mohammed Ali).

An example relating to American history:

THE TEACHER IN AN ELEMENTARY SCHOOL is discussing General Custer and the Battle of Little Bighorn. The next day, the students (who are about 12 years of age) are asked to paint pictures relating to the event. They pick up their brushes and depict General Custer on his horse, Indians with arrows, fighting soldiers, and similar scenes. One boy, however produces a strange picture: at the top is a fish with a halo and below it a lot of copulating Indians. The teacher is shocked and confronts the boy: "This has nothing to do with American history. Nothing at all. It is incredibly nasty. I will have to call your parents."

The boy answers: "Why doesn't it have anything to do with American history and the Little Bighorn? General Custer said: 'Holy mackerel! These fucking Indians just keep coming and coming!'"

Multiply Partiality

Multiple partiality, or neutrality, is a principle in family therapy. It says that the therapist should not side with one member or one part of the familiy, but must maintain a neutral position.
The following well-known story is a perfect example of this attitude.

A RABBI, WHO IS ALSO THE VILLAGE JUDGE, frequently holds court sessions in his living room. One morning, he is visited by a very excited villager who describes the crimes his neighbor has commited. The rabbi listens to him until he's finished and says: "You are quite right."

Not two hours later, the neighbor himself appears. He tells the rabbi in great detail about all the wrongs the first villager has perpetrated. Again the rabbi listens to him until he has finished and then says: "You are quite right."

The rabbi's wife, who has been following these events from the kitchen, enters the living room and takes her husband to task: "Are you out of your mind? You tell the first party: 'You are quite right.' Then, when the second party comes along, you also say: 'You are quite right.' That's not the way you're supposed to handle it. You can't just do that!"

The rabbi considers this for a while, and then says: "You are quite right."

Seen from a different perspective, the following story also sheds some light on the principle of multiple partiality.

A MAN IS HIKING IN SWITZERLAND. High up in the mountains, he happens on a small pasture. There he sees a farmer. Two cows are grazing in the meadow. The hiker wants to strike up a conversation with the farmer and says: "You've got two very fine cows there."

The farmer answers: "Oh yes, the white cow is really a model cow. Just look at her face and notice the wonderful markings on her coat." He carries on enthusiastically for a while and the hiker says: "And the brown cow? Isn't she also a lovely cow?"

The farmer: "Ah, yes. The brown cow, actually the brown cow is also a very lovely cow."

The hiker pursues his subject: "Do they also give milk?"

There's no stopping the farmer now: "Well, the white cow, she is such an unbelievably good milk cow! She gives at least 30 to 40 quarts a day. That is unbelievable. Especially the quality of the milk, the cream content . . ." The wanderer interrupts him: "Ah, I see, the brown cow isn't such a good milk cow?"

The farmer: "Well now, she is. Actually, the brown cow is also a very good milk cow. She also gives 30 to 40 quarts of milk a day. And the cream content is also excellent."

The two continue talking about this and that for a while. The hiker gazes around him and eventually says: "You've got quite some slopes here. You probably can't use agricultural machinery. Do you use your cows to work in the fields?"

"Oh," says the farmer, "I don't like using such good milk cows for field work. But if it can't be avoided — well, I can tell you, the white cow is very obedient, she is very clever. The way she pulls the plough, it is a real treat.

The wanderer says: "Aha, so the brown cow isn't really suited for field work."

The farmer: "Actually, the brown cow is also very clever and obedient when pulling the plough."

Rather amazed, the hiker interrupts the farmer: "Now, I feel I do have to point out something. You are always praising the white cow, but it seems that the brown cow is just as good."

"Well," says the farmer, "it's just that the white cow is my cow. You have a different relationship with an animal that you call your own."

"And to whom does the other cow belong?"

The farmer: "Ah, the brown cow. Actually, the brown cow is also my cow."

(Note: This beautiful story about the two cows was told to me by Kris Klajs, the director of the Polish Milton Erickson Institute.)

Natural Healing Versus Modern Medicine

Some view the blessings of modern medicine with a critical eye and many turn to other cultures' natural healing practices. The following story shows why they do.

A TOURIST RETURNS HOME from a trip to the Far East. A short time later, he discovers that he's contracted a strange venereal disease. He goes from one doctor to another and listens in growing dismay as they all advise him to have his penis amputated. Desperate, he inquires about natural healers. A natural healer in China is recommended to him. It also seems logical that one should consult an Eastern doctor about an Eastern disease. He flies to China and visits this well-known Chinese natural healer. The healer examines him and the patient asks anxiously: "Must my penis be amputated?" "No, no, no," replies the Chinese doctor in an assuring and convincing tone. The patient smiles in relief: "Do you know, all our Western doctors say it has to be amputated."

The Chinese doctor frowns and looks perturbed: "These Western doctors. It's always operate, operate, operate. Just wait another two weeks and your penis will drop off all by itself."

The Ordeal Technique

The ordeal technique stems from Milton Erickson.
  The client is given a therapeutic assignment whereby putting an end to the symptoms seems more attractive than carrying out the assignment. For example, a patient suffering from insomnia is assigned to polish his floors for a couple of nights. How Erickson chanced upon the possibilities inherent in this method is known only to a few people.

A MAN CONSULTS ERICKSON FOR ACUTE BRONCHITIS. Erickson examines him and prescribes some medication.
  A week later, the man returns for a follow-up examination. Before the patient enters the consulting room, Erickson glances at the man's chart and notices, to his dismay, that he had prescribed a laxative by mistake.
  He apologizes at once. But the patient says: "Don't worry, Doctor, it worked really well. I was afraid to cough after taking the medication."

The Overlapping Technique

The overlapping technique is a term derived from NLP that describes a technique Milton Erickson used to intensify hypnotic experiences. The therapist steers the imaginative processes by starting with one sense and increasingly involving other channels of sensory perception: "While you are seeing this picture, what are you hearing . . . ?" This would be typical of the phraseology used to intensify an experience. The imaginative processes become more vivid with such instructions. Filmmakers employ this method by supporting the images on the screen with background music.

THERE ARE THE TWO PRETENTIOUS WOMEN who attend a new opera that has recently opened. One woman says: "I think that there are bad acoustics here." The other one pauses for a moment and then answers: "Now that you mention it, I can also smell them."

TO ADD A FINISHING TOUCH TO THE OPERA EPISODE, I'd like to continue my musical discussion. Did you know that Beethoven was so deaf for a large part of his life that he thought he was a painter?

>(Note: In German, the punch line is funnier because the German word for painter is "Maler," which is pronounced the same as the composer "Mahler.")

Pain Control

Pain control, one of the classic subjects in clinical hypnosis, entails the employment of ancient knowledge possessed by all cultures before the discovery of anesthesia. (Note: There is a famous book on hypnosis that describes many surgical procedures carried out using hypnotic anesthesia: Esdaile, J. [1850]. Mesmerism in India and Its Practical Application in Surgery and Medicine. Hartford, CN. *Also, an excellent overview of contemporary approaches using hypnosis for pain control is given by: Barber, J. [1996].* Hypnosis and Suggestion in the Treatment of Pain. *New York: Norton.)*

Impressive examples of pain control without a formal induction are also known.

A MISSIONARY IN AFRICA is determined to convert a particularly wild tribe. The colonial army, currently stationed in the same region, repeatedly warns him to give up this idea — but to no avail. The missionary is set on bringing his message to these people. The officer in command of the military base bids him farewell and informs him that he and his men will form a search party to look for him if the missionary is not back in two weeks. When the missionary hasn't returned in that time, the commander gives marching orders. The beating of the drums gets louder, the nearer the troops draw to the tribal settlement. Obviously, there's a great feast going on. The soldiers advance silently under cover of the night and see the missionary tied to a stake and with a spear protruding from his stomach. They fire a few salvos into the air and the natives disappear into the underbrush. The commanding officer advances toward the missionary. In the sympathetic manner generally attributed to the military, he addresses the victim: "That must be terribly painful" (see pacing, mirroring of emotional experiences). The missionary answers: "Actually, only when I laugh."

Some people have the natural ability to apply pain-control techniques.

A PROFESSOR OF BIOLOGY AND TWO STUDENTS are living outdoors in the wilderness in order to find and study rare plants. They are sleeping together in a tent. In the middle of the night, they hear a sound outside. The first student feels obligated to see what is going on. He slips out of the tent noiselessly and, after a short time, a loud "boing!" fills the air. Then all is quiet. The student returns and the three are almost asleep when again a strange sound is heard in the night, and the other student goes outside. A while later, a "boing!" rings out, followed by a hush settling over the area. When later another sound breaks the silence, the professor bravely crawls outside. In a moment, a "boing!," followed by another "boing!" in quick succession, resounds through the darkness. One student turns to the other and whispers: "Didn't I tell you that the professor would probably step on the rake twice."

Pain Control:
Dissociation and Diverting Attention

We don't know the technique employed by either the missionary or the professor of biology, but one of the central techniques in pain control is the diversion of attention. One focuses one's attention on something else (e.g., a pleasant recollection, a piece of music, the voice of the hypnotist), resulting in dissociation from pain.

A basic technique of this procedure is illustrated by the following story from Isaac Asimov.

MR. JONES HAS BEEN HAVING PROBLEMS with his teeth and he goes to see a dentist in New York. The dentist checks his teeth and announces: "This looks like it calls for a complete treatment of your entire mouth. Of all your teeth." Mr. Jones is astonished and says: "A complete treatment?" The dentist answers: "Yes, all the teeth on the top, as well as on the bottom, both back and front. It will cost between $10,000 and $12,000. It can't be done for less." The patient is shocked and says that his insurance doesn't cover such a large amount, but the dentist remains firm, saying that nothing can be done for under $10,000.

However, he adds that a younger dentist had set up practice a few years earlier a couple of blocks away, and that it might be a good idea to get a second opinion, as the younger doctor might charge less. Mr. Jones sees the other dentist, who also recommends a complete treatment that includes all his teeth, but his estimate is only $6,000. The patient says that naturally he is interested in saving such a large amount of money, but the quality of the treatment is equally important. The young dentist understands his patient's concerns about the quality of his work as compared with that of the older, more experienced dentist. So he tells Mr. Jones: "Two years ago, I had a patient whose treatment was similar to the one you need. He's a very nice person. I'll give you his number and you can ask him whether he was satisfied with my work."

Mr. Jones phones the former patient. He is indeed a very open person and seems willing to tell Mr. Jones what he wants to know. But instead, he starts talking about his hobbies. Mr. Jones interrupts him in the hope of gaining the information that will help him decide which of the two dentists to choose.

Ignoring the interruption, the former patient continues to talk about his regular morning jog. After a while, Mr. Jones interrupts him again and mentions his dilemma concerning the dentists. The former patient consoles him once more, adding that he will give him the information in his own time. He goes on, saying: "And do you know what I most look forward to every morning? After jogging for about half an hour, I always come to this lonely little lake. With the day just dawning, I take off my clothes and enjoy a solitary swim, completely naked. There is something incomparably appealing in this act. Sometimes a light mist seems to hover over the lake. Then, about 14 days ago, I was just coming out of the water when I suddenly saw a young woman swimming there as well. She was striking out toward the shore. I must say, I felt quite embarrassed! There I was, completely naked, standing on the shore with no place to hide, my clothes lying at least 30 feet away. And can you imagine? The woman was also completely naked. What's more, she wasn't the least bit embarrassed about it. She just came toward me and greeted me with a quick kiss. And the minute our bodies touched, for that one brief moment, it was the first time in two years that my teeth didn't hurt at all."

Part of the Whole

The proportionate part of the whole is a subject that psychotherapists encounter in many different ways — in systemic theories, in philosophy, in ecology, Gestalt psychology, and so on.
This subject becomes clear in the following anecdote.

A SAILOR IS ADMITTED TO THE HOSPITAL. Nurse Heidi appears in the nurses' room shortly afterward and excitedly reports: "The new patient is in his room washing himself, and his entire body is covered with tattoos — even his penis." The other nurses express their doubts. But Nurse Heidi is adamant. She maintains that the sailor had a word tattooed on his penis. She said the word was "Hot," or something like that. Nurse Helen is very curious and can't let the matter rest. She also goes to the new patient's room and returns after a while. "I agree with you to a certain extent, Heidi, but only partly," she says. "His entire body is definitely covered with tattoos, even the part you mentioned. But the tattoo there doesn't say 'Hot.' It says 'Honor and Glory to the Baltic Fleet.'"

Just how important the subject of the part and the whole is can be seen in the extraordinarily numerous variations on this joke, including versions with Adam and Amsterdam and swan and Saskatchewan. In yet another version, the word tattooed on the penis is reported to be "Wendy," but after further investigation, it turns out that it is really: "Welcome to Jamaica, and have a nice day."

A MAN GOES TO A DOCTOR AND COMPLAINS: "Doctor, no matter where I touch, it hurts terribly. Here, for example: Ouch! Or here: Ouuuch. It's terrible." And wherever the man even lightly taps his finger, he yells with pain. The doctor conducts a thorough examination. After evaluating the results, the doctor puts the man's mind at rest: "Don't worry. You've only broken your forefinger."

I'd like to close this section on "the part and the whole" with the following question: "What is the most insensitive part of the penis?" Answer: "The man."

Pattern Interruption

Some modern psychotherapeutic techniques are based on the interruption of long-standing behavioral patterns. This principle, which was employed by Milton Erickson, also is utilized by his students. Steven de Shazer, for example, gives his most stubborn problematic clients a homework assignment: "Be it ever so crazy, do something completely new by the next session." Even the stutter-therapy pioneer, Charles Van Riper, has stutterers replace their customary "uh, uh, uh" with "oh, oh, oh," or even "umba, umba" temporarily. (Note: See Van Riper, C. [1984]. Speech Correction. Englewood Cliffs, NJ: Prentice-Hall.)

That's why I have asked myself whether the following joke is really a joke, or is simply the report of a professional conversation held in an anteroom at a solution-oriented conference.

Two psychotherapists meet: "Do you know," says one, "I generally start each treatment by asking whether the patient plays chess. If he or she does, then I forbid the patient to play it anymore. If the patient can't play chess, I prescribe it."

"Yes, but what for?" asks the other. The first one answers: "I've no idea, but it's always worked so far." (Note: Ericksonian therapists use an advanced version of this approach. They tailor treatment and so modify the technique and prescribe — or forbid — bridge, poker, or other games.)

Prophylaxis

Therapist: "Alcohol makes one indifferent."
Patient: "I don't care."

Psychohistory

Lloyd de Mause proceeds on the assumption that political and social behavior can be traced back to changes in the various educational styles over time. De Mause postulates that in the course of the last 2,000 years, the attitude toward children has become more tolerant.

This is evidenced, for example, in Germany as well. Sixty years ago, it might have been said: "When a German father comes home, even the walls seem to pull themselves together." The remarkable changes that have taken place are illustrated in the following story.

A FATHER IS SITTING AT HIS SON'S BEDSIDE and they are singing songs together. The father then picks up a book of fairy tales and starts reading aloud. His son says: "Dad, could you read in a lower voice? I'd like to go to sleep now!" (See multigenerational perspective.)

A few days later, the two go for a walk in the woods. The son sees an interesting little bird: "Oh, Dad, look! What kind of a bird is that?" But the father doesn't know the answer. The boy spies some mushrooms. "Oh, what kind of mushrooms are these? Can one eat them?" Dad answers: "I'm afraid I don't know." "What kind of a tree is that? Dad, look at those berries, what are they called?" Dad doesn't have an answer to either question. Finally, his son remarks: "I shouldn't ask you so many questions, should I? It gets on your nerves, doesn't it?" "No, no," his father reassures him. "go ahead and ask. After all, I want you to learn."

The following scene took place in an upper-class family a few decades ago.

THE WIFE URGES HER HUSBAND to undertake the sexual enlightenment of their 17-year-old son. The husband, however, feels that this is a mother's duty. Eventually, his wife persuades him that, according to tradition, this special topic should be handled by the father.

The man calls his son aside and begins: "You are now 17 years old, and I have to talk to you about a few things." He thinks for a moment, and then continues: "Do you remember when the two of us visited Paris two years ago?" "Yes, Dad." "Well, do you remember when we met those two women one evening?" "Oh yes, very well." "Do you remember what we did with the two women?" "Of course." "Well now, you see, it's about the same way with the birds and the bees."

Like so many other things, the idea of sexual enlightenment has changed. The following episode demonstrates just how much.

EIGHT-YEAR-OLD BILLY seeks out his father one day during his school vacation and asks: "Dad, where did I actually come from?" The father, who is raising his son alone, feels his blood pressure rising. He's been preparing himself for this moment for a long time and now the hour of truth has arrived. He calls his office and says that he'll be at least an hour late due to a child-raising issue. He explains to Billy in detail the basic elements of how he was conceived, making everything plain and lucid. The boy listens to him fascinated, his eyes growing bigger. After about half an hour, the father asks: "Now, have I answered your question? Is everything clear?" The son says: "No, not really. You know, yesterday at the playground, Toby told me he comes from New Jersey. So where do I actually come from?"

Psychosocial Imprinting, or Job-Related Illnesses

Many vocations involve typical job-related illnesses, such as pneumoconiosis. Sometimes a therapist assumes the role of healer and doctor, sometimes the role of teacher, sometimes that of companion or jester. The kinds of job-related illnesses that psychotherapists risk are evident in the following story, which sheds some light on the personality structures of social workers, and psychotherapists, and teachers respectively.

TWO MEN ARE SHOT DEAD IN A GUNFIGHT, a common event in the old Wild West. The two widows debate on how to carry on without their husbands, and decide that their best bet is to open a brothel. They rent a three-story house and hire several women. As expected, business is good, but within a few weeks, they begin to notice an odd phenomenon. Business on the first floor is great, on the second floor it is OK, but almost nothing is happening on the third floor. The brothel owners are at a loss. As far as they are concerned, all three floors, and their hostesses, are equally appealing, and yet there is no denying the fact that the amount of business they attract differs greatly. One day the women are discussing this puzzling problem over dinner in a local restaurant. An elderly gentleman sitting at the next table overhears their conversation. He has patronized their establishment several times, and he interrupts them: "I can tell you why business on one floor is very good while on another it is almost nonexistent. And I will explain to you what the trouble is, but only if you promise not to change anything, no matter what happens." This leaves the two proprietresses in a bit of a predicament. Naturally, they want to remedy this baffling situation, but they're also anxious to discover the reason. Finally, their curiosity gets the better of them. They make their promise, and the man explains: "You know, the women on the first floor are former ranch workers, salesclerks, and the like. There is always a great atmosphere on this floor. It is very relaxed. And above all, if a man has a problem making it happen, it's no big deal, it just didn't work. He will come back again the next day, and then it will work out better. Everyone takes it easy. On the second floor, things are a bit different. Former social workers and psychotherapists work there. And when a man experiences difficulties, they always know the reason and what can be done about it. Well, some men like that, and some do not. Now as for the third floor, that's where former teachers work. If a man cannot perform, they say: 'And now, my dear, you will stay here and practice until you get it right.'"

(Note: The person who told me this joke added that Virginia Satir had told it at a workshop.)

MANY, MANY YEARS LATER and many thousand miles away, the Berlin Philharmonic is giving a concert with Herbert von Karajan as conductor. After half an hour, someone in the first row stands up and shouts: "Is there a doctor in the house? Is there a doctor in the house?" Von Karajan loses some of his composure and his musicians almost lose their rhythm. Then, once again, the man shouts: "Is there a doctor in the house?" A man in the back stands up and calls softly: "I'm a doctor. What in Heaven's name is the matter? Is there an emergency down front?" The man in the first row shouts back: "From one colleague to another, isn't it a wonderful concert?"

At intermission, two psychotherapists meet and one says to the other: "How am I? I can see how you are."

And at the Berlin railway station, not far away and at almost the same time, the following takes place: a tourist gets off the train and asks directions of a passerby, who happens to be a psychotherapist. She answers: "I have no idea, but isn't it good to have been able to talk so openly about it?"

Reflexivity – Circularity – Circular Causality

These concepts are important in the fields of cybernetics and systemic theory. They concern a sequence of causes and effects that lead back to the initial cause. This subject can best be elucidated by the old question: "Which came first — the chicken or the egg?"

I found the following jokes on this topic.

TWO SWEDES STOLE A TRUCK LOADED WITH BRANDY. And what did they do with the brandy? They sold it. And what did they do with the money? They spent it on booze.

A TRAVELING MISSIONARY has been proselytizing to many wild tribes in the course of his journey. One day, however, he goes too far when he seeks out a tribe of cannibals. The cannibals take the live missionary and stick him into a pot of soup. Suddenly, the chief's little son rushes to his father, highly excited: "Father, Father, come quickly, the missionary's eating up all the rice in the soup!"

Circular processes also played a role in the following episode.

A MEMORIAL CROSS HAS BEEN ERECTED on a mountain famous for its echo. Someone asks the guide the reason for the cross. He explains that it was put up in commemoration of a female tourist who went out of her mind on this spot. She always had to have the last word.

Maybe the next episode is a shade too complex.

MARY AND JOSEPH ARE ON THEIR WAY TO BETHLEHEM. Joseph is tired. He is distracted for a moment and steps into a hole, spraining his ankle. "Jesus!" he mumbles into his beard. Mary turns around and positively glows: "That's a good name for our child."

(Note: Another version is: "That would be a wonderful name for our baby. Don't you think it's better than Kenneth?")

Charles Van Riper, the speech-therapy pioneer, described how, owing to his passion for gardening, he lost three fingers in a compost machine. He then scattered the compost over his pea field, thus recycling himself. He did add that not everyone is lucky enough to be able to smell and taste his or her own immortality in this way.

Reframing

Reframing is a term used to describe the transforming offer of a new frame for one's mode of thinking. A picture can have a different effect and look different when put in a new frame. A situation can also be perceived in a different way if someone offers a new frame. The Iranian doctor and therapist Peseschkian once reframed the frigidity of a woman patient, saying: "You've got the ability to say 'no' with your body." Family therapy and Ericksonian hypnotherapy both use these reframing techniques in a variety of ways.

A reframing can also involve a change of view, and reveal a surprisingly new perspective, as the following story shows.

As EVERYONE KNOWS, everything is bigger, faster, and better in the state of Texas. For instance, it is said that one Texan, upon seeing Niagara Falls, muttered: "In Texas, a water main break like this would have been repaired ages ago." And so it goes that another Texan, while traveling through Europe, visits the Black Forest (where I come from) and strikes up a conversation with a farmer. This farmer is mighty proud of his farm — his piece of the forest, his fields, and his meadows. But the Texan is contemptuous. "Have you ever been to Texas?" he asks. The farmer says no. "Then I'll tell you what it's like in Texas," the American says. "In Texas, I get into my Ford pickup at 7 o'clock in the morning, and take my hunting rifle and my wife along. Then we drive westward, ever westward. In the evening, we stop for a break, and resume our journey very early the next morning. Again we drive westward, not once changing direction. In the afternoon, around 4 o'clock, is when I'll have reached the boundary of my ranch. That is Texas, boy, Texas."

The Black Forest farmer says: "Oh dear, oh dear! I used to have a car like that." (Note: Stephen Gilligan told me this joke during the first European Congress on Ericksonian Hypnosis and Psychotherapy in Heidelberg in 1989.)

A HOBO WAS TRAVELING through the same region of Germany a few years earlier. He rang the doorbell of one of the houses and an old woman looked out of the top window. "Ma'am," he complained, "I haven't eaten in three days." The old woman answered: "Well, you just have to force yourself."

(Note: Recently I found a different punch line. The old woman says: "I really would like to have your willpower.")

WE'LL LEAVE THE BLACK FOREST altitude and descend into the lowlands of the circus arena. The circus is giving a night performance. IDs are checked rigorously. The performance starts at 11 p.m. The circus has been becoming less and less popular. With the advent of satellite TV, striptease has become commonplace and just isn't exciting anymore, even if performed on a tightrope. While some spectators make wisecracks, like we could at least see a double somersault, the lights suddenly dim and the spotlight lands on the ringmaster. He announces the debut of a unique presentation, a trained crocodile. The trainer enters and gives a signal. A huge crocodile slowly starts moving toward him. Just before it reaches him, he signals it to stop and the crocodile stops. The trainer stretches his left arm out horizontally before him and folds his right arm over his left so that his hands are folded. With small abrupt motions, his arms start to move apart (see arm levitation). In accordance with these movements, the crocodile starts opening its jaws with small jerky movements. The audience is spellbound (see focused awareness). Finally, the tamer lets his right arm rest at an angle of 45 degrees pointing upward. His left hand moves toward his crotch, where he opens his fly and places his penis between the crocodile's jaws. Then his two outstretched arms start moving toward each other again with abrupt little motions. The crocodile slowly and jerkily starts closing its jaws once more. The audience is absolutely motionless (see catalepsy). The jaws have almost closed. Breathtaking suspense. At the last moment, the tamer delivers a blow to the crocodile's head with lightning speed. The crocodile wrenches its jaws open (see rapid reorientation). Thunderous applause. The response dies down. The tamer solemnly zips up his fly and strolls over to the microphone: "$10,000 for whoever will repeat this performance!" Nobody moves (see indirect reinduction of catalepsy).

After a while, the tamer says: "OK, I'll give another demonstration." Once again, he folds his arms, and then opens them slowly and with jerky movements. As he does so, the crocodile opens its jaws. Once again, the tamer places his penis between the crocodile's jaws before slowly inducing the crocodile to shut them. This time, the tamer takes it to the limit. At the very last moment, he delivers a lightning blow. Thunderous applause. He casually zips up his fly, and strolls toward the microphone: "$20,000 to the person willing to repeat this." Again, the audience sits motionless. But there seems to be a movement at the back, where the cheap seats are. The tamer seems surprised. Never before has anyone dared to accept his offer. An old woman comes down the aisle and enters the ring. The tamer greets her, slightly shaken and a bit at a loss. The woman seizes the opportunity and starts explaining that she's very embarrassed, but her pension is very small and she'd be prepared to try the stunt for $20,000. The tamer seems quite confused. The nonchalance with which he had zipped up his trousers just minutes before has deserted him. The situation seems to be getting out of hand. If he hadn't lost his feeling for the events taking place in his pants (see dissociation), he would have noticed that his penis was erect because it was too short to hang down.

Finally, the tamer regains his composure to some extent and says to the little old woman: "But, dear lady, that won't work. There is a certain small difference between a man and a woman." Before he can finish what he has to say, the old woman reiterates that she is willing to try it at all costs because of the smallness of her pension. Before the tamer can decide what to do, the woman takes the microphone out of his hand and says: "Could I ask a small favor though? That you wouldn't hit me on the head quite so hard?"

(Note: What really amazes me is the fact that nobody ever predicts the punch line. In some way, "castration anxiety" seemed to block the listener's ability to change direction.)

Reincarnation Therapy

During reincarnation therapy, clients recall past lives while in trance. One of the reasons for doing this is to find the causative factors responsible for present-day problems by probing into past-life memories. Another concept of reincarnation is that rebirth into this life is connected to things that were left unsolved or with lessons not learned in former lives.
This is illustrated by the following story.

As a child, a man had witnessed a great flood. Now, he repeatedly recounts this experience to his relatives and friends, who have become fed up with hearing about it. Eventually, the man dies and goes to Heaven. Saint Peter welcomes him and tells him that in Paradise he can do as he pleases, whatever his heart desires. The man's immediate wish is to deliver a speech on the great flood. Finally, everything has been arranged and the hall is packed. Just before the speech is about to begin, Saint Peter hands the man a note, which bears the message: "Strictly between you and me, Noah is in the audience."

From what I've heard, the above happened shortly before a renewed reincarnation. In his new incarnation, this person is supposed to have driven his parents and several therapists to despair with his persistent bed-wetting.

Rigid Belief Systems and World Views

Rigid belief systems and world views of patients and clients can pose a problem for the therapist. Alas, clients are often reluctant to let go of their beloved conceptions. Thus, Milton Erickson believed that one should not approach these belief systems directly.

The following stories shed light on this problem.

A PATIENT IS CONVINCED THAT HE IS ALREADY DEAD. All of the doctor's attempts at trying to persuade the man otherwise are unsuccessful, even though he has pointed out that the patient's body temperature, respiratory functions, and many other factors corroborate the fact that he is alive. Finally, he asks the patient: "Tell me, do corpses bleed?" The patient answers: "Of course not!" The doctor takes a needle and pricks the patient's thumb. The thumb starts bleeding. The doctor remarks: "And now, what do you say to that?" The patient answers: "I was mistaken. Corpses do bleed."

But rigid views of life don't play a part only in the clinical arena. The following event took place in the U.S. South at a time when the rights of African Americans were not respected.

THE SHERIFF IS ON HIS REGULAR PATROL when he finds the corpse of a black man in a ditch, riddled with 24 bullet holes. He turns to his deputy and mumbles: "In my entire career I've never before seen such an extreme case of suicide."

Role-Playing Theory of Hypnosis

An old discussion in the field of hypnosis centers on the question of whether a hypnotic state is really a different state of consciousness. Some researchers claim that a hypnotized person only acts as though in a trance state. The fact is that even experienced hypnosis specialists like Milton Erickson couldn't distinguish between a person who is acting as though hypnotized and one in an actual trance state during a controlled experiment.

The following story is supposed to have taken place a few days before the role-playing theory of hypnosis was established.

A SPECIALIST IN HYPNOSIS who later became quite famous received a phone call from an old friend: "I'm worried about my father. He's been suffering from insomnia for the last few weeks and is getting weaker by the day. We've already tried everything: warm beer, valerian, psychopharmaceuticals, monotonous music, and so on. We've even forced him to stay awake for hours, but nothing seems to have helped so far. Can you hypnotize him?"

The hypnotist agrees to do so. At the friend's house, he holds up a pendulum, has the father focus his attention on it, and starts talking.

"Your eyes are feeling tired and heavy, very tired and very heavy. More and more. Tired and heavy. And your eyes close. That's right. And you sink deeper and deeper into a pleasant, comfortable, heavy tiredness free from time and space." The hypnotist's voice becomes increasingly monotonous, mirroring the old man's breathing, which is also becoming more relaxed and even. After 40 minutes, the hypnotist gradually comes to the end of the session: "You will sleep for a long time and enjoy a restful and well-deserved sleep, and the next few nights, you will remember the pleasant drowsiness and my voice and sink into a deep sleep, quickly and safely."

The hypnotist gets up and quietly leaves the room. At the door, he beckons to the son sitting on the other side of the bed, signaling him to also leave the room as quietly as possible. The son is just about to rise when his father opens one eye and asks: "Has the crazy nut gone yet?"

Search Process

In hypnotherapy, the therapist tries to trigger "search processes" in the client's mind with regard to finding solutions to problems. For instance, the therapist tells a story, the meaning of which is not obvious at first. The client then searches for the meaning behind the story, trying to make sense of it. This entails the client's own inner search processes and interpretation, and often turns up amusing and innovative personal solutions.

Such search processes often occur in everyday life, as can be seen by the following event that took place some years ago.

A HUGE PASSENGER SHIP is on her way to the United States, passing through icy northern waters in the middle of winter. Her rudder is blocked and the ship is slowly drifting toward a huge iceberg. Most likely, the ship will be torn apart upon impact. The captain sends for a passenger and informs him about the situation: "I know that you're a world-famous magician, and you are our only means of salvation. In about 30 minutes, the ship will probably be torn apart by an iceberg. But there is no reason to panic as other ships have already altered their courses and are heading toward us, and should arrive in time. Our problem is that all our passengers are in the ballroom at the moment and panic will inevitably break out if they learn of the situation too soon. It could lead to extremely foolhardy reactions: people may get trampled to death, lifeboats could be damaged, some might even jump overboard in panic. Please go into the ballroom and give a spontaneous demonstration. Stage a show to keep the people occupied so that no one will even think about going outside to stand at the rail. Perhaps the other ships will arrive soon. If they don't and the impact is imminent, I will give you a signal and you'll announce that your next number is the biggest stunt you've ever pulled off, namely, that you will make the ship break into two parts. Before the people realize that it's not a clever magic trick, but reality, we will have the biggest hazard — panic breaking out — under control and most of them will be sitting in lifeboats."

The magician does as requested. He makes cards disappear, reads thoughts, and performs other tricks. In short, he holds the passengers spellbound. Half an hour passes and the captain gives the prearranged signal. The magician says: "And now, for my last magic trick, and also the highlight of this show, I will make this ship break into two parts and we will all proceed to the lifeboats." He makes a wide sweeping gesture with his arms. A violent jolt passes through the ship, followed by a terrible tearing sound. In just a few minutes, the ship is submerged in the water and most of the passengers are sitting in the lifeboats. Other ships have also arrived and are busy rescuing the passengers, most of whom are too confused to be afraid. The magician is waiting at the rail until he can board one of the few remaining lifeboats. He is shivering with cold. One passenger, already seated in the lifeboat, turns to him with a slightly dazed and confused look and asks: "Aren't you the magician? Now what was supposed to be the trick of the matter?"

This story would have long been forgotten had it not been for two missing passengers. One of them had managed to save himself by climbing on top of the concert piano floating about at sea. The other one swam toward him, asking: "May I accompany you?" After a couple of hours of aimlessly floating about in the freezing ocean, the two were able to climb onto a huge iceberg. Suddenly, one nudged the other: "Hey, we're saved! Look, there's the Titanic up ahead."

Seeding

The concept of seeding was derived by Jay Haley from Milton Erickson's work; Jeffrey Zeig compared it to the sociopsychological concept of priming. To cut a long story short, before Erickson ever made any recommendation or suggestion, he had intimated it, and smoothed the way for it, long beforehand, so that it would fall on fertile ground.

This is illustrated by the following two stories — the first in a subtle way, and the second more obviously.

A MAN SUDDENLY COLLAPSES AND DIES WHILE PLAYING GOLF. Nobody wants to be the one to break the news to his wife. Finally, the dead man's best friend agrees to do it, as he is also acquainted with the wife. He phones and says: "Karen, your husband lost over 7,000 playing poker." Karen: "What? I'm going to kill him!" The friend: "Oh, no need."

THE SECOND STORY TAKES PLACE IN THE BED OF A STOCKBROKER. The stockbroker wakes his wife and says: "The stocks are rising. Don't you think this is a good time to jump in?"

His wife turns over and says: "The stock exchange is currently closed."

The broker turns away, visibly disappointed.

After a while, his wife turns toward him again, and whispers: "Darling, the stock exchange is open. I'll take everything you'll sell."

He answers: "Too late, I've already squandered them single-handedly."

It's a pity that the stockbroker wasn't familiar with the concept of seeding and the time factor — in this case, the typical time delay concerning the acceptance and transformation of suggestions — as the whole affair would have been more productive.

Self-Hypnosis

TWO WORKERS NEARING RETIREMENT are talking about their sex lives. One bemoans his impaired potency. The other says he can't complain and that the previous night he'd had sex with his wife three times in short succession. His friend is incredulous and asks him whether he took any medication. "No," says the other, "I learned self-hypnosis. I had sex with my wife and then went into a short, deep trance for 10 minutes, telling myself that I'd wake up totally refreshed, and then I made love to my wife again, went into another short, deep trance, and had sex a third time."

The other worker is fascinated and immediately signs up for the recommended course. He learns the art of self-hypnosis and is advised just to go into a deep trance at first and then to reorient himself. A short time later, the man decides to try out his newly acquired knowledge. He sleeps with his wife and goes into a deep trance. He reorients himself, has sex with his wife, goes into a deep trance again, and emerges refreshed and ready for a third round. Satisfied, he goes to sleep. He oversleeps the next morning though, and arrives at work 20 minutes late. His boss is waiting for him at the main entrance, a frown on his face. "You're late," he says, stating the obvious. The man can't hide his chagrin and answers: "For the last 27 years, I've been reliable and I've always arrived for work on time, and now you're making a fuss over 20 minutes?" "What do you mean, 20 minutes?" says his boss. "Where were you on Tuesday and Wednesday?" (See time distortion in trance.)

(Note: One of the best books about self-hypnosis is: Alman, B., & Lambrou, P. Self-hypnosis. The Complete Manual for Health and Self Change. New York: Brunner/Mazel.)

Shifting of Symptoms

The shifting of symptoms is a psychoanalytical concept based on the assumption that by spiriting symptoms away in a superficial suggestive manner (without considering deeper causes), other symptoms can emerge.
The following story sheds new light on the question of why Freud later spurned hypnosis.

A MAN IN HIS MID-40S CONSULTS FREUD, complaining that he's been wetting his bed for the past few weeks. He has a recurring dream. A little green man is sitting at his bedside, urging him in an intense voice: "You have to pee, you have to pee! You will pee, and you will pee! You will pee and pee. Pee. Pee!" And, then, he says, he wakes up to find that he has wet his bed. Freud hypnotizes the man and plants the suggestion that during his dream he will recite: "I don't have to pee. I won't pee. I'm not peeing," to the little green man.

The man returns for the following session and says: "It's gotten even worse. I had the same dream again. Before the little green man had a chance to say anything, I said: 'I don't have to pee, I won't pee...' That's when the little green man interrupted me, saying: 'Who said anything about peeing? You have to shit, and you will shit...'"

What the next joke has to do with a shifting of symptoms is not quite clear.

What is the ultimate rejection?
When you are masturbating and your hand falls asleep.

Short- Versus Long-Term Therapy

A controversial question in the discussion surrounding psychotherapy is the one concerning its duration. The following story (told to me by Harold Mosak) sheds some light on this question.

A MAN SEES A PSYCHOANALYST: "I think I'm going crazy. Every night I see and hear wild animals — lions, tigers, elephants — parading beneath my bed."
 The analyst: "Lie down on the couch over there and tell me more about it."
 The patient: "Just a moment. How much will it cost and how long does such therapy take?"
 The analyst: "One hour costs $100. The therapy will take at least 80 hours, with the possibility of continuing for another 80 hours if necessary."
 The patient: "I'm not that crazy."

A FEW WEEKS LATER, the psychoanalyst and the would-be patient happen to meet at the supermarket. The analyst asks the man how he's doing.
 Patient: "Oh I'm fine. My brother-in-law cured me in less than an hour."
 Analyst: "And is your brother-in-law also a psychotherapist?"
 Patient: "No, a carpenter. He simply sawed the legs off of my bed."

Side Effects

As yet, there are still no "prescribing information" leaflets warning of possible side effects that might be caused by an individual therapist, or by a whole therapeutic school of thought. Perhaps such leaflets could be written in code so that clients would have to start doing some thinking of their own in order to spot the weaknesses of their therapists and the possible side effects.

For psychoanalysts: "Forever lasts the longest." Or for the solution-oriented short-term therapist: "I had a solution, only it didn't fit the problem." Or as Jeff Zeig said after a therapy demonstration that didn't quite work out: "Excellent technique but the wrong client." Or, finally, for the future-oriented therapist: "At the edge of an abyss, progress is a step back."

Now something on the subject of side effects in general.

AT LEAST THIS PATIENT who visits his doctor complaining of feelings of weakness doesn't have any problems with side effects. The doctor prescribes a well-tested and proven tonic. He is very confident that it will be effective and the following week he asks the patient in a self-assured manner: "And how did the tonic work?"

The patient: "I'm afraid I can't say. I wasn't able to open the bottle."

At this point, systemic therapists would probably quote Heinz von Förster to the effect that a human being is not just a machine, and one can never predict what exactly will ensue after an "intervention."

THIS INSIGHT ALSO SET A CLERGYMAN to thinking when he sent a paralyzed member of the congregation to the Holy Spring of Lourdes. The handicapped man drove his wheelchair into the healing waters, only to reemerge with the wheelchair equipped with four new tires.

Often, a patient even chooses to risk any possible side effects. Being aware of this greatly relieves the therapist of responsibility. This is illustrated by the following two stories. (Note: These jokes are from one of my favorite joke books, J. Pietsch's The New York Cab Driver Joke Book.)

A MAN WITH BADLY BULGING EYES has been seeking help from plastic surgeons for years. But no doctor will perform the surgery because of the possible risk of causing blindness. The man is frustrated and unhappy. All the women he meets say: "You're a nice guy but I can't ignore your bulging eyes." So the man spares no effort in looking further for a willing surgeon. Finally, he discovers one in Argentina and flies there. The doctor points out that the operation entails considerable side effects. The patient is nervous and anxiously asks the doctor about the kind of side effects he should expect. The doctor describes the operation as follows: "We have to remove your testicles and then your eyes will sink back into their sockets. But I can readily assure you that you will look absolutely great."

The patient departs, indignant: "Where's the advantage in that? Why do you think I want to have this operation in the first place?"

Unfortunately, the years pass and no woman is able to look past his popping eyes. So the poor hero of our story decides to undergo the operation after all. "At least I'll be good-looking then" is his razor-sharp conclusion. And indeed, shortly after the operation, his eyes sink back into their sockets and an imposing, striking face looks back at him from the mirror. Because of the low prices of custom-made clothes in Argentina, he asks for a recommendation of an excellent tailor and looks him up. He selects the best materials for suits, shirts, leather jackets, hats, and shoes. The tailor: "You can collect everything on Thursday." The customer: "I don't think you really understand what I'm after. I'd like custom-made suits, shirts . . ." The tailor interrupts him: "I do understand. Everything will be ready by Thursday."

"Yes, but don't you want to take my measurements?" The tailor smiles mildly: "I've had 20 years of professional experience. I can take your measurements at a glance." Our customer seems skeptical, so the tailor recites his measurements for him, proving his infallible eye. "You wear a size 16 collar, right? You've got a size 35 waist, right?" He continues with the man's hat size, shoe size, length of sleeves. The tailor obviously enjoys demonstrating his experience and skill. He goes on: "You wear large-size shorts!" This time, the customer interrupts: "Now you're mistaken. I wear size 'small' shorts!" The tailor: "I've had more than 20 years of experience. The size you wear is 'large.'" The customer: "But I wear 'small.'" The tailor: "You can't fool me. If you were wearing 'small' underwear with those trousers, your eyes would come popping out of your head like a frog's."

In the following story, the witch also duly pointed out the side effects of her prescription, but her "client" opted for them.

A VERY AMATEUR GOLFER is playing so badly that he has to search for his ball in the woods and he gets lost. Finally, he happens upon a witch and laments about his pitiful golf experiences. She has mercy on him and offers to sell him a magic potion that will enable him to master the game. However, she points out that the purchase does have side effects: "Your love life," says the witch, "will be lousy after taking the potion." But being a typical man, playing golf is very important to him. He requests the drink, and sure enough, he begins to play golf like a professional. Within a few months, he's ranked the no. 1 amateur golfer in the world, the celebrated shooting star . . . on the golf course. A year later, he remembers the witch and seeks her out to tell her of his success. The witch gently tries to remind him of the price he has to pay for all this, but he keeps on recounting his victories. Finally, the witch interrupts him and says: "But in exchange for all that your love life is lousy." He answers: "Actually, I can't complain." The witch: "Don't tell me any fibs, I know how this magic potion works. How often have you slept with a woman this year?" The golfer: "Three or four times." The witch: "And you don't call that having a lousy sex life?" "You know," says the golfer, "as a Catholic priest with a relatively small congregation, I really can't complain."

Stage Hypnosis

During stage hypnosis, hypnotic phenomena are put to improper use in order to entertain. In some countries, stage hypnosis is forbidden and is a punishable offense. The following story shows why this is so.

A YOUNG MAN DISCOVERS THAT HE HAS A TALENT FOR HYPNOTISM. He has a few posters printed announcing a hypnosis show to be held in the hotel at a spa. On the day of the show, the hall is packed. He asks six volunteers to come up on stage and uses his valuable old pocket watch as a pendulum. The volunteers go into a deep trance and the young man, delighted, decides to hypnotize the whole audience. He descends from the stage and wanders through the auditorium with his watch in hand, and virtually the entire audience goes into trance and complies with his every suggestion. The young hypnotist hurries back to the stage and trips, smashing the old pocket watch that's been in his family for generations. He reacts automatically. "Shit," he says loudly. Ten days later, the cleaning staff is still busily scrubbing the hall.

In order to make ends meet, considering all the damage claims, the young man decides to rent the small theater in a neighboring town and present a modified version of his show. "I can heal all ills and afflictions," he shouts at his audience. "Does anybody have an ailment?"

"Yes, I have," answers an old man on crutches, "I can hardly walk."

"Lame one, come on stage, you shall be helped. Is anyone else disabled or handicapped?"

One other man, who has a harelip, responds. The hypnotist directs the two men: "Go behind the folding screen."

The hypnotist turns toward the screen and starts talking in a suggestive tone of voice. The spectators are mute with suspense. "And now, lame one, throw away your crutches!" The crutches come sailing over the folding screen.

"And now, you with the harelip, say something!" Complete silence.

"Once again, man with the harelip, say something!" A voice rings out from behind the screen: "The wame ome has just fawen on his fwace!"

(Note: Karl-Ludwig Holtz, a well-known professor and child psychologist from Heidelberg, added this joke while proofreading the German version of this book.)

Strategic Therapy

Strategic therapy describes the working procedure of a therapist who plans therapeutic moves a few steps ahead. Strategic procedures exist everywhere in life, as can be seen in the following story about a wedding night.

THE CEREMONY OVER, the wedding festivities seem to go on forever. The remaining guests just don't want to leave. The bride has spent the last hour longing for the intimacy of the honeymoon bedroom and her wedding night. Eventually, the party comes to an end. The bride and groom are standing in front of the bed at last. The bride's mind is filled with tender thoughts and she feels the desire and need for the love and tenderness for which she has been waiting so long. Suddenly, her husband's trousers come flying toward her, grazing her head. (Note: Ernest Rossi and other hypnosis experts call this "disrupting the conscious set of expectancy.") The bride, dismayed: "What's that supposed to mean?" The groom: "Put on those pants!" The bride is astonished, but her husband becomes quite intimidating and aggressively orders her to put on the trousers immediately. Bewildered and disenchanted, she puts on the trousers. But no matter how hard she tries to tighten the belt around her waist, the pants are too big and end up falling down. At last, the groom is satisfied: "Just so you know right from the start exactly who wears the pants in the family and whom they fit."

WHILE A FAMILIAR TUNE starts playing in the bride's head and she starts humming "Don't marry, be happy," her new husband sees a certain game of poker pass before his mind's eye. One of the married card players would always become more agitated, the later it got, and finally would go home in order to avoid another domestic quarrel. His plan would be to park the car a block away, sneak into the house via the back door, get undressed in the kitchen, avoid turning on the lights in the bedroom, and then crawl into bed without disturbing his wife. But usually she would wake up and nag him endlessly. Another card-playing buddy was aghast at this description of what, to his mind, was a totally ineffective strategy. He explained that on late nights like these, he would blow his car's horn a block away, thunder into his garage, close the garage door with a bang, storm up the stairs, run into the bedroom, turn on the lights, and say: "Well, how about tonight?" This ensured that his wife would pretend to be asleep.

BUT LET'S GET BACK TO THAT WEDDING NIGHT. As the groom smugly contemplates the poker game scenario while taking off his shirt, his wife's panties whiz past his ears (reorientation from a common everyday trance and simultaneous focusing of awareness, as an experienced hypnotherapist can effortlessly discern). The bride: "Put on the panties!" The husband, slightly confused: "Why?" The bride: "Listen, I put on your trousers, now put on my panties!" (Notice the polite and more indirect technique used by the wife as compared with the husband's somewhat authoritarian approach.) The groom attempts to don the panties, but it's impossible. He is too thickset. "I can't get into your panties!" The bride answers: "That's right. And you won't ever get into my panties if you don't change your attitude."

> *To what extent the previous story relates to strategies can only be assessed by a skilled specialist because, a few years later, the following episode involving the same couple took place.*

IT IS 7 O'CLOCK IN THE MORNING. The wife is fuming, waiting for her husband to come home. He hasn't shown up all night. Then, a few minutes later, he arrives on their doorstep. She confronts him, haggard from lack of sleep. "And how do you propose to explain your way out of this?" He answers: "Now don't get all worked up! There was this conference at work and it dragged on into the night. I was absolutely furious with those idiots. That's no way to work effectively. My secretary had missed her last train, so I offered to drive her home. During the ride, I was so upset about the way the conference had gone that I nearly had two accidents. My secretary tried to calm me down and said that I should not be driving in the state I was in. She invited me in for a cup of coffee. After all that excitement, I felt too tired to drive home, and my secretary offered me her sofa to sleep on. Then . . ."

His wife interrupts in a fit of temper: "How can you lie to me so shamelessly? You know you spent the whole night in your office trying to install that new program in your computer."

The Structure of Magic, or "The Communication of the Masters"

Structure of Magic is the title of a book by Grinder and Bandler. The inventors of NLP assumed that neither witchcraft nor sorcery was involved in the astoundingly successful results achieved with almost magical swiftness and sureness by the masters of psychotherapy. They believed, instead, in underlying principles that can be taught and learned. They analyzed and interpreted the forms of communication used by "the old masters of the trade," such as Erickson, Perls, and Satir. Later, this method of analyzing complex therapeutic behavior was also applied to other masters of communication. However, according to some psychotherapists, interpretation was often stretched too far, resulting in an overemphasis on the magical aspect of communication.

The following story was handed down by Isaac Asimov. It shows the difficulty involved in trying to follow the complex verbal and nonverbal communications of the real masters. The story reminds one of the old proverb: "Everything in the world has a meaning that goes far beyond itself."

ROME, IN THE MIDDLE AGES: The Pope is determined to banish the Jews. The situation is escalating. A civil war seems imminent. The Pope offers to conduct a public debate with a Jewish representative. If the Jews win the debate, they may stay; if the Pope wins, the Jews will have to go. But not one of the rabbis is prepared to take part in the debate. They all think it's silly to become involved in a discussion in which the Pope not only is a participant, but is the referee as well. Finally, the janitor of the synagogue agrees to enter into the debate with the Pope. At first, the rabbis are against his proposal as it doesn't seem fitting for a man in his position to represent them in such an important matter as a discussion with the Pope. But as nobody else seems to be willing to confront the Pope under these conditions, they eventually consent.

The day of the debate arrives. But the Pope seems to be having second thoughts about the whole idea. He isn't sure whether he can win against the Jews, who have been schooled in the Talmud. He is aware of their rhetoric versatility and their ability to use paradox. As the Pope can determine the rules of the game, he decides that the entire debate will be conducted nonverbally.

The debate begins:

The Pope clenches his fist and energetically points his index finger toward the sky. The janitor of the synagogue points his finger toward the ground in the same energetic manner. The Pope reacts at once and again points his finger skyward. The janitor lifts his right hand and holds up three fingers. The Pope seems to be at a loss, but after a moment's hesitation, he dips into his coat pocket and comes up with a round, red apple, which he displays to the people.

Without hesitating, the janitor reaches into his coat pocket and somewhat awkwardly pulls out a bag. He opens the bag and takes out a matzo. The Pope bows his head and says: "You have won." He retires to the company of his shaken cardinals. "I am sorry," he says, "but the man was extremely quick at repartee, he is a master of debate. I had no chance." The cardinals ask him what it was all about. None of them had been able to follow the debate and not one had understood the discussion. The Pope analyzes the event: "It was perfectly obvious. I pointed toward the heavens and said: 'There is only one God.' My Jewish opponent replied by pointing his finger toward the ground, and thus saying: 'But there is also a devil in hell.' And what could I say to that, considering that it is also part of our own Catholic belief? Then I said: 'But God is mightier.' And my Jewish colleague answered with three fingers erect, meaning: 'But only because it is the Father, the Son, and the Holy Ghost, namely, the Holy Trinity.' And what, pray, could I say to that other than it is also our belief? Then I thought I'd lead him astray and showed him an apple as a symbol for the erroneous belief that the earth is a globe. And what does he do? He shows me his matzo and thus implies that, in reality, the earth is a disk. And that was when I knew I had lost."

The rabbis, though, are also nonplussed and at a loss concerning the course of the debate, especially the almost magical speed with which the janitor had been able to tilt the scales in their favor. They ask him how he did it. The janitor says: "In my opinion, the whole thing was a hoax. First, the Pope showed me his fist with the index finger raised. This being a threat: 'You will all be thrown out of Rome.' Then I showed him that we will definitely stay. So he raised his fist and pointed his index finger skyward again, saying: 'You will still be thrown out of Rome.' So I indicated to him: 'Even if you repeat it three more times, we will still stay.' Then what does he do? He reaches into his coat and shows me his lunch. So I show him my lunch as well."

(Note: From Asimov, I. [1971]. A Treasury of Humor. *Boston: Houghton Mifflin.)*

The Structure of the Outer Interaction Becomes the Structure of the Inner Dialogue

The Russian psychologist L. S. Wygotski conceived the psychological concept of the structure of the outside interaction becoming the structure of the inner dialogue. Thus, the way in which one speaks to and associates with a child reflects how the child will address others and handle himself or herself in later years.

Let's take a look at a story from this perspective.

THE WORRIED MOTHER is having a discussion with her best friend about the problems she's having with child rearing: "I think I'm too strict with Christopher." Her friend asks her the reason for this assumption. "Well," says the mother, "not long ago, on his third birthday, I took him to the fair. Then I lost sight of him and had to collect him from the police station. He'd told the police that his name was Christopher Stopthat."

THE SON OF A MAFIA BOSS must have had a similar experience. Night after night, he knelt before the picture of Jesus: "Dear Lord Jesus, please see to it that I get a racing bike!" This went on day after day, but his wish was not fulfilled. Finally, the boy sneaked into a church and stole a statue of the Madonna. He wrapped and tied it up carefully and hid it in his parents' attic. Then he knelt before the picture of Jesus once more: "Now, dear Lord Jesus, if you ever want to see your mother again . . ."

Symbolism

A look at the history of humankind shows that symbols have been used for countless centuries. A totem pole, a cross, a national anthem, a coat of arms, they are all examples of symbols. Psychotherapists also make use of symbols to set processes of change into motion effectively.

THESE TWO NATIVE AMERICANS must have been confused about the strange symbols they came across in some smoke signals. Upon discovering a barbecue area, one said to the other: "It smells better than over at our place." The other replied: "Yes, but it doesn't make any sense."

Symmetric Escalation

If, in a relationship, each party continually tries to dominate the other, the result is symmetric escalation. Family therapist Helm Stierlin used the boxing term "clinch" to describe very advanced stages.

THE APPROPRIATENESS OF THIS COMPARISON was noticed by a small boy while watching a boxing match on TV. When the program was over, he said to his father: "They can teach you and Mom a thing or two. At least they shake hands at the end."

A short while later, the couple visits a family therapist, who turns to the woman during the first session and asks: "You say that you two have been in a clinch for the past 15 years. When was the first time you and your husband had a really big fight?" The woman answers: "The first time was when he absolutely insisted on being in the wedding photo." (See also related individuation.)

A few clinch-years later, the partners find themselves before a judge in a divorce court. The judge turns to the husband: "Your wife accuses you of not having spoken a single word to her for two whole years. Is this true?" The husband answers: "Yes, I didn't want to interrupt her."

Some couples manage a soundless and grim clinch by employing mutual silence, as the following joke shows.

THE COUPLE HASN'T EXCHANGED A WORD for the last two weeks. Notes are used to communicate messages that are absolutely necessary. The wife is in bed when her husband receives a business phone call telling him to fly to a very important meeting in Sweden early the next morning. The alarm clock is in their bedroom, but the husband has sworn not to enter the room until his wife apologizes for whatever was the cause of their quarrel. But he knows that his wife has to get up early in the morning to go to work, and so he leaves her a note: "Please wake me at 6:30 tomorrow morning as I have urgent business in Stockholm and have to take the first flight out." He stirs at 8 o'clock and is jolted awake when he notices that it's already light outside. Then he sees the note on his bedside table: "It's 6:30, time to get up."

Some couples manage to enrich this personal clinch perspective with a contemporary macho-feministic perspective.

SO HE PROVOKES HER WITH THE QUESTION: "What does a real man do when his wife doesn't have an orgasm?" and immediately gives the answer: "Nothing, because a real man doesn't care." She retorts: "What is the definition of too small?" and then adds: "Is it still inside?"

Readers may find comfort in this sentiment: "It's a good thing that the custom of marriage exists, otherwise we'd probably have to fight with complete strangers most of our lives."

Tailoring Interventions

Tailoring is a technical term in Ericksonian hypnotherapy that refers to adjusting the therapeutic procedure to the client's individual personality. Trance induction, therapeutic stories, or homework is tailored to fit the specific situations. How this term came into being is shown in the following.

A MAN ORDERS A CUSTOM-MADE SUIT FROM A TAILOR. When the suit is ready, the customer goes for a final fitting. But he's less than satisfied with the result. He tugs at the sleeve, motioning to the tailor that the length is wrong. The tailor says: "Yes, considering the way you're standing, it's no wonder. But at some point, you'll probably want to give a speech and make a sweeping gesture, something like this." The tailor makes a sweeping gesture and asks the customer to do the same.

"See? The sleeve fits perfectly," he says triumphantly. "OK," says the customer, "but what about the trouser legs, they seem so sloppy and wide. Just look!" The tailor: "Well, if you stand like that, of course. But if you bend your leg at an angle — a little bit more — as though you're at a cocktail party, casually leaning against a wall. Exactly! Now see how well the trousers fit."

The man pays for the suit and leaves the shop wearing it, his arm held in that sweeping gesture, his right leg bent at an angle even when walking. Two women watch him. One whispers to the other: "Look at the poor crippled man over there!" The other replies: "Yes, but he's got a first-rate tailor."

Technological Advances in Medicine

A MIRACULOUS NEW DIAGNOSTIC MACHINE is demonstrated at a medical conference. The machine apparently can diagnose any kind of physical problem just by analyzing urine. The doctors are delighted because they finally will have more time to spend on consultations. One doctor immediately orders the new machine, and when it arrives one evening, he unpacks it at once, studies the instruction manual, and makes all the necessary adjustments. Then he urinates on the test strip, inserts this into the machine, and a few seconds later, a pleasant voice announces: "The diagnosis is tennis elbow, the diagnosis is tennis elbow." The doctor is annoyed at such nonsense. A machine certainly can't diagnose tennis elbow just by analyzing urine. He is so incensed that when he gets home, he collects urine from his 17-year-old son, his 15-year-old daughter, and his wife. The next morning, he mixes the three samples of urine together and then adds his own urine and that of his dog. Arriving at his office, he pours the mixture on the test strip and inserts it into the machine. A few seconds later, the pleasant voice announces: "Your dog has distemper, your daughter is pregnant, your son is homosexual, your wife has a lover, and if you don't give up masturbating, your tennis elbow will get even worse."

Time

Time is an important factor in our culture, and so it is also important in psychotherapy. The Sigmund Freud 50-minute watch already exists for therapists, as do short-term and single-session therapies. And soon, we will probably have ultra-short-term therapy as well.

Even primary school students are made aware of the importance of the time factor, as the following shows.

THE TEACHER ASKS THE CLASS: "Which travels faster, light or sound?" A student answers immediately: "Sound." The teacher: "What makes you say that?" The student answers that whenever he turns on the TV at home, sound is the first thing to emerge, and the picture appears later. The teacher says: "I'm afraid that was a wrong answer."

Another student raises her hand: "Light travels faster." "Right! And why?" The student thinks about it: "When I press the power button on my stereo, the lights come up first, followed by the sound." The teacher says: "Right answer, wrong explanation. Once again, which travels faster, light or sound?" A third student pipes up: "Light." The teacher asks for the reason behind the response. "When I stand on a mountain and a shot is fired on the opposite mountain, the first thing that appears is the smoke from the gun, and only later can the shot be heard." Before the teacher can praise the boy, reinforcing him psychologically, he adds: "And that's because our eyes are closer to the front than our ears are."

The teacher deliberates for a moment (see also search processes, acquired helplessness, premature retirement, and similar key words) and decides to address the subject "faster" one more time, but this time from a fundamental point of view.

So he asks the question: "Now children, what does 'fast' really mean? Give a few examples!" Charlie raises his hand and says: "Well, when I travel from Baltimore to Washington by train and it takes an hour, then that's fast." Sally puts her hand up: "Yes, but when I fly from Washington to New York and that takes an hour, that's much faster!" "Excellent!" praises the teacher. Sebastian raises his hand. The teacher can determine by the look on the boy's face that he can expect a unique answer: "If the chickens are as flat as the plaster, once again, the tractor was faster." To restore the class to order, the teacher turns to Mollie. Mollie is the daughter of a philosopher and can always be counted on for a well-thought-out answer. Mollie opens her atlas, traces the distance between New York and Moscow with her finger, and says: "When I travel from New York to Moscow in my thoughts, then that is the fastest. Nothing is faster than a thought." The teacher enthusiastically lauds little Mollie. But Freddy intervenes excitedly: "That's not true! Just a few days ago, I was listening at our neighbors' door and heard the man say to his wife: "Hey, I came faster than I thought."

Triangulation

Triangulation is a family-therapy term that implies that when two persons have a conflict, they tend to include a third party. This third person can be a therapist, a child, a friend, or anyone else.

A special case of triangulation can be seen in the following.

THE HEAD OF THE PSYCHIATRIC WARD gives a tour of the facilities. The visitors are allowed to look into a room where a somewhat confused-looking man is sitting on a chair clutching a life-sized wooden doll with blond hair made of straw that is sitting on his lap. He continuously cuddles and kisses the doll. The physician analyzes: "This man was deeply in love with a blond woman many years ago, but she married another man. He then transferred his love to the doll, believing it to be the woman." They continue their tour. The room next door is completely padded and the patient inside is banging his head against the wall, uttering heartrending moans. The visitors ask: "And what's wrong with this man?" The physician answers: "That's the man who married the woman."

(Note: This joke is from a book of jokes related to mental illness that is no longer available. The author was Prof. U. H. Peters, former president of the German Psychiatric Association.)

Turning Weaknesses
Into Strengths

This an interesting principle in Ericksonian psychotherapy. Erickson himself was an example of this attitude. Many hypnotherapeutic techniques that were developed by him resulted from his overcoming his illnesses and handicaps. He suffered from polio, didn't speak until he was four years old, was partially color-blind, and had arrythmia, as well as dyslexia. He knew from experience that illnesses and handicaps can be important resources for becoming familiar with the nature of different states of consciousness and their healing possibilities. This principle of searching for strengths and resources in so-called weaknesses can be seen in many of Erickson's case studies. For example, a young woman wanted to commit suicide. She considered herself too unattractive to ever find a man. She thought her problem might be the gap between her two front teeth. Erickson motivated her to practice the following daily in her bathroom. Fill her mouth with water and squirt it through her two front teeth until she could squirt over a distance of at least six feet. The woman had once mentioned a man who would arrive regularly at the drinking fountain at work at the same time she did. Erickson told the woman to squirt through her teeth at the man from a distance of six feet, and then run away. She did, and the man ran after her and briefly held her in his arms. The next day, he hid near the fountain with a water pistol, and squirted it at the woman when she appeared. He then asked her out to dinner. The two got married soon after, and the topic of suicide never came up again.

This principle was employed in a creative way when Jeff Zeig visited Israel a few years ago. He went to dinner with colleagues in the evening. The light in the restaurant was dim and Jeff couldn't read the menu, which was in small type. He became a bit annoyed at this. A companion said: "It's not the light or the size of the letters. It all has to do with growing older. You need glasses." Someone gave Jeff a pair, but he still couldn't read the menu. He related the following story.

A YOUNG WOMAN IS IN AN UNFAMILIAR CITY ON BUSINESS. The shops are closed, and she is feeling bored, all alone in her hotel, so she decides to go for a walk. Soon, she finds herself in a red light district, standing before illuminated letters proclaiming: "Sex show. For adults only. ID check." She thinks about it for a moment, and then decides to give herself the pleasure of experiencing a show like this for once. The program proves to be unusually tasteful and very creative. A number toward the end is really inspiring. A young, extraordinarily well-built man comes on stage and performs a very classy striptease. Finally, he is completely naked. The stage is dark, except for a spotlight focused on his well-muscled physique. Unexpectedly, a second light appears, which is trained on a small table. The table is carried to the middle of the stage and an attractive assistant arrives with a walnut, shows it to the audience, and places it on the edge of the table. The dancer steps up to the table. He stands spread-eagled, holding the palms of his hands at head level. His eyes close briefly, a short moment of concentration, a focusing on the walnut, and then — a cry followed by a cracking sound. The man had cracked the nut with his penis. The applause is deafening and the woman is very impressed. She tells her husband about this unbelievable performance when she phones him in that night. Back home, she relates the experience to her friends, and even tells her children about it when they get older.

Twenty-five years later. As fate would have it, the woman visits the same city again. The scene from so many years before is still etched on her mind and she's curious to know whether the nightclub still exists. With a bit of effort, she finds the street, and, believe it or not, the place is still there. Not only that, but the striptease artist has taken over the club and performs his act as the main attraction every evening.

As before, he comes on stage and does his striptease with a masterly elegance. He is still well built and in very good shape. At the end, the table again is carried onto the stage, and the assistant arrives — but this time with a coconut. A roll of the drums, the hands held at head level, a moment of concentration, the cry — and the coconut is split.

The woman is just as enthusiastic as she was the last time. She waits until the place is almost empty and then addresses the maestro. She tells him that she had seen his show once before, 25 years earlier, and that now, as then, she found it very exciting. Moreover, she is very impressed by the fact that he has developed his talent even further, going from splitting a walnut to splitting a coconut. The owner of the club says: "Well, 'develop' depends on how you see it. I'm 25 years older now and my eyes aren't what they used to be."

Utilization

According to utilization, one of the core concepts in Ericksonian hypnotherapy, not only should the central characteristics and peculiarities of clients be analyzed and diagnosed, but an attempt should be made to utilize these toward therapeutic goals. Example: a psychotic thinks he's Jesus. Erickson talks to him: "I hear that you've had some experience as a carpenter." Erickson then instructs the man to build a bookcase for the clinic.

This principle is sometimes used intuitively by parents and vocational counselors, as the following story shows.

THE PARENTS TAKE THEIR LITTLE SON, Max, to a vocational counselor and have him tested. Afterward, the counselor talks to them. "Does your son have any special preferences or abilities?" "He likes animals so much," says his mother, "we've considered that the vocation of butcher might be just the thing for him."

Real estate agents have also heard of this principle.

THE REAL ESTATE AGENT is busily extolling the virtues of a property up for sale: "With these residential premises, you will gain a huge advantage. Not too far north there's an oil refinery, a fishmeal factory to the south, a chicken farm to the east, and a garbage dump to the west." The prospective buyer is somewhat aghast and asks: "And where is the huge advantage in that?" The realtor: "You'll always know exactly which way the wind is blowing."

During therapy, some clients not only learn self-hypnosis and other skills needed to achieve their goals, but some incorporate the principle of utilization in an almost brilliant manner, as the following story shows.

A STUTTERER TURNS UP AT A BIBLE SOCIETY and offers to sell Bibles door-to-door. "I wwwwwwannnt tttto ssssssell BiBiBibles." It takes him more than half a minute to utter only this one sentence. The manager at first refuses to use his services. But the stutterer is very persistent and repeats over and over again: "Bbbbut I wwwwannnt tttto ssssell BiBiBibles." Sometimes it takes him longer, sometimes it takes less time to get his message across.

The manager gives in and hands him two Bibles and two invoices. The stutterer protests: "Nnnno, I wwwant ttttto sssssell ttttten BiBiBibles." Finally, the manager gives him another eight Bibles and an invoice pad. At about 10:30 a.m., the stutterer leaves the office of the Bible Society. At about 5:00 in the afternoon, he returns, carrying the money he received for the 10 Bibles and the invoice duplicates. The manager is very surprised, and the stuttering young man takes 20 Bibles the next day. He returns at around 3:00 in the afternoon, having already sold all the Bibles. The manager says to him: "I've been the manager here for 13 years. Never before has anyone managed to sell more than seven Bibles in two days. How do you do it?"

The stutterer explains: "Thththat's qqqqqquite eassssy. I rrrring thththte ddddddoorbbbell. And thththen I ssssay I've ggggot a BiBiBible hhhhere. Wowowould yyyyyou llllllike me ttttto rrrread yyyou an exxxxxxxccccerppppt or wowowould yyyyyou lllike tttto buy one?"

(Note: The idea of using this joke to illustrate the utilization approach comes from Kasia Szymanzka, Codirector of the Polish Milton Erickson Institute.)

Voluntary Versus Involuntary Movements

In hypnotherapy, an important distinction is made between the terms "voluntarily" and "automatically." We can move an eyelid deliberately, but usually this happens automatically. In the same way, we can breathe deliberately, but, for the most part, our breathing functions regulate themselves.

Hypnotherapists often work with such voluntary happenings: for example, arm levitations or ideomotoric finger signals, which means that an arm or a finger has moved involuntarily without being controlled.

To illustrate such involuntary movements as vividly and realistically as possible, we've spared nothing. Hours and hours of research using the worst possible joke books as information sources, as well as field studies, paid off in the end. This time we will do without certain jokes just to raise the standard for a while. The hypnotherapist knows this procedure as a fractionated technique.

TWO ROOFERS ARE WORKING ON A ROOF. It starts raining and they soon slide down the roof together. They can both barely hold on to the rain gutter. The ground is seven stories below. The gutter was never meant to support such a heavy load and it slowly begins to curve downward: it's only a matter of time until the two men won't be able to hold on any longer. At the height of their predicament, one of them proposes: "I think it is time we folded our hands in prayer."

A COMPLETELY DIFFERENT PROBLEM CONFRONTS JOHN WAYNE as he rides through the West desperately searching for a public rest room. He heads for the only saloon in town, tethers his horse, and hurriedly enters the barroom. He asks the bartender: "Excuse me, but do you have stalls in your lavatory, or is it one common room?" The bartender answers: "I'm sorry, we only have an open room." In some distress, John Wayne rides on. The same thing happens in the next town, there are no stalls there either. In the third town, John Wayne enters the saloon gingerly and slightly stooped, and asks his question. The bartender responds that as far as he knows, there aren't any rest rooms with stalls in the entire area. John Wayne sighs and says resignedly: "Oh well, what must be, must be." He enters the rest room, reappearing a short time later. His right trouser leg is thoroughly wet and his left trouser leg is completely soaked. The bartender: "Oh God, what happened to you?" John

Wayne: "It's always the same. I am standing in front of the urinal and the man on my left and the man on my right simultaneously turn toward me and ask in unison, 'Aren't you John Wayne?'"

We can learn from John Wayne that our chances of being urinated on definitely increase in direct proportion to our degree of fame.